INNOVATIVE FACULTY
TEAM PROGRAMS:

AN ADMINISTRATOR'S HANDBOOK

INNOVATIVE FACULTY
TEAM PROGRAMS:

AN ADMINISTRATOR'S HANDBOOK

By

Raymond Clarke

Parker Publishing Company,   West Nyack, N.Y.

© 1977, by

PARKER PUBLISHING COMPANY, INC.

West Nyack, N.Y.

Library of Congress Cataloging in Publication Data

Clarke, Raymond
    Innovative faculty team programs.

    Includes index.
    1. Teaching teams. 2. School management and
organization. 3. Open plan schools. 4. Individualized instruction. I. Title.
LB1027.C4696   371.1'48   77-8674
ISBN 0-13-465674-1

Printed in the United States of America

DEDICATED

to

THE STUDENTS OF WEST ELEMENTARY SCHOOL
CULLMAN, ALABAMA

FOREWORD

In the milieu of our changing world there is a great thrust toward educating the total child to meet the demands of our technological society. Schools are often viewed with a critical eye because they have not prepared man to meet these needs. No doubt, many educational programs do have gaps which leave them open to such criticism. Yet, in the midst of cries asking why Johnny can't read or spell or write, there are educators chiseling away at the hard, cold facts, structuring programs to meet the needs of each child.

In educational circles many new approaches have been proposed and implemented, some of which are good and others in need of improvement. Some dissatisfied educators and parents, however, are demanding a return to the traditional approach without even allowing these newer, more innovative systems to be tried by the fire of teachers' enthusiasm and good teaching. It seems that the major emphasis by these few still focuses on mass education, group training, and total group productivity.

As each child is different, so the path to learning is different for every child. Raymond Clarke feels that the dignity and value of each child is of utmost concern. Because of his belief, Mr. Clarke offers this contribution to the field of education. His approach sees the child as the initiator and center of his own learning. The teacher, particularly when working as part of a modern, faculty *team*, is the facilitator and guiding hand, drawing forth a desire for beauty, joy, and

3

learning. This facilitator does not stifle innate abilities such as creativity or imagination, but rather channels these individual gifts toward their fullest potential,thus enhancing the whole person and enlarging the self-concept.

In his book, Mr. Clarke exhibits a sensitive concern for the community and the role of the school in society. He sees a need for flexibility in the school program based on sound educational theory to meet the needs of the community. Throughout his book he stresses this together with his basic philosophy that the individual child must be brought to a realization of his personal responsibility for self-direction and development of a good self-concept. This achieved, our Twentieth Century society may yet see community needs met through joyful fulfillment of individuals.

The author offers practical suggestions for systematic changes involving students, faculty, parents, curriculum, and the physical plant. He is convinced that change can take place regardless of the financial status of the school or system—the key to his basic understanding is: "Success is attitude."

Sister Mary Adrian McLean

THE SCOPE AND PRACTICAL VALUE
THIS BOOK OFFERS

Innovative Faculty Team Programs: An Administrator's Handbook is a book of tested guidelines for administrators who want *practical* ways to revitalize their school or school system. It contains a broad range of tested, common sense approaches to many of the most disturbing problems facing educators today.

Cooperative planning through faculty teams transcends by far the earlier concept of team teaching. Cooperative planning has become a means to an end rather than an end in itself. Not only has cooperative planning served as a vehicle for curriculum planning and professional development; in our school, it has become an effective vehicle for shared decision-making as all the teachers are jointly involved. Out of this cooperative team effort a realistic instructional program evolved, along with appropriate management systems, and it has the the virtually unanimous support of the entire staff. For example, one such management technique was developed by the staff through a cooperative team effort, making it possible for teachers to completely individualize math instruction quickly . . . and effectively. This technique, which has been successfully applied in other subject areas, is described in depth in Chapter Eight.

Every program described in this book has been thoroughly tested, and based upon the resulting success our school was designated as a model for the nation by the United States Office of Education. One of the major reasons for the success of this program is that classroom teachers were able to perform as an efficient *team*, without the need for complex management systems which often require the use of computers or other forms of elaborate equipment.This program's effectiveness has attracted a large number of visitors from all parts of the nation as well as visitors from foreign nations.

Here are several compelling examples that illustrate the accomplishments of this school as it moved through a systematic faculty team plan designed to effect basic changes.

* A complete transition from the self-contained classroom to a team approach with semi-open classroom was realized. This resulted in providing the flexibility needed for implementing a completely individualized instructional program and provided for cooperative team planning.

* A completely individualized instructional program was developed in the skill areas of reading and math, utilizing a diagnostic prescriptive approach. One of the major benefits was that teachers were able to diagnose the *specific* skill needs of each child, and curriculum materials were organized in such a manner that the programs were manageable.

* A structured but relaxed learning environment has replaced the more formal classroom setting, although essential controls have not been relinquished. An important by-product of this has been that both students and teachers enjoy a higher morale, for learning has become exciting and relevant.

* Diagnostic testing centers have been organized and put into operation. These centers are manned by paraprofessionals. This has freed the teachers of clerical tasks and allowed them to work more closely with students in an instructional capacity. Also, the traditional stigma attached to tests has been removed. Students no longer dread tests, for they have become diagnostic in nature and are not used to indicate the child's degree of success and/or failure.

* Positive attitudes have emerged, replacing earlier confusion on the part of some parents, teachers, and students

regarding the school's programs. This has likewise resulted in increased morale which has in turn brought about increased productivity.

* Students have become more involved in their own learning which has helped to promote more self-direction. This has brought about increased achievement as noted in the validation report.
* Special education classes have been mainstreamed with gratifying results. Because of this, parents no longer object to their child working with the special resource teachers, and the students do not object, for the stigma which has traditionally been attached to special education classes has been removed.
* The library has evolved into a unique media center which serves as the heart of the instructional program. This has resulted in a wider, more productive use of instructional materials.
* The concept of failure and/or promotion has evolved into a third alternative. Rather than being failed or promoted, each child works on a given skill until it has, indeed, been mastered . . . and then moves to the next skill. Grades have given way to parent-teacher conferences and/or narrative reports.
* Grouping of students has ceased to be any major concern, for students are grouped across grade lines. As you begin to deal with children as individuals, then the group no longer matters. In some instances this has made it possible to divide all students evenly among the teachers, and teacher units have been reduced.

Administrators searching for practical ways to bring about similar changes in their school or school system will find a wealth of specific information in this book. The procedures, accomplishments, and problems encountered during the change process will be described in detail and effective programs along with practical alternatives will be proposed. In Chapters Two and Three, realistic procedures have been spelled out showing effective ways to modify the attitudes of reluctant teachers who wish to maintain the status quo, or of parents who fail to perceive the need for changes.

Most of the suggestions found in this book will require little or no additional funding, and they will enable you to start from where you are in taking full advantage of current resources found in every classroom. The programs and activities have been used very effectively in the open-space, non-graded classrooms as well as in the self-contained, graded classroom.

Whether you are a principal desiring to change the school environment, a supervisor attempting to upgrade curriculum, or a superintendent wishing to move an entire school system ahead, you will find these ideas to be challenging, realistic, and most of all, effective. When the ideas in this book are used, they will help you make your school a place where children spring to life as they strive, with increasing success, to develop their potential.

Raymond Clarke

Acknowledgements

The author gratefully acknowledges the contribution of each of the following and the part they played in making the educational innovations described in this book a success. Without their assistance this book could not have been written.

The entire West Elementary School Staff, past and present, whose hard work, dedication, and determination made the project a tremendous success.

The West Elementary School parents for their understanding and unrelenting support during many trying hours.

The Cullman City Board of Education, who recognized the need for change and provided the necessary encouragement, support, and freedom for the West Elementary School Staff to accomplish its objectives.

Dr. Arthur W. Dennis, Superintendent of Education, and his staff, whose unyielding support and understanding proved invaluable as the programs described in this book were developed and implemented.

Dr. Lanny R. Gamble, Director of Extended Services at the University of Alabama, who served as the Title III ESEA Project Director in Cullman City Schools at the time of implementation and whose unyielding support and assistance proved invaluable.

Dr. J. Foster Watkins, Professor at the University of Alabama, who worked with us under the auspices of the Southeastern Educational Laboratory and in his former role as Associate Dean of Education at Auburn University. His influence played a major role in the innovations discussed in this book.

The State Department of Education, whose advice, assistance, and support was most beneficial.

Dr. Azalia Frances, Educational Director at Athens College, who served as our Title III ESEA Educational Program Auditor, rendering valuable assistance to our total effort.

And to the following individuals who helped with editing and typing the manuscript: Jorene Kinser, Imogene Mayo, and Linda Schgier.

CONTENTS

Organization of Diagnostic Tests and Testing Centers . . . Format for Organizing Curriculum Materials . . . Management Systems for Monitoring Pupil Progress . . . Recommended Implementation Procedures . . . Accountability Techniques to Insure Proper Implementation.

Identification of Basic Areas of Concern in the Language Arts Program . . . Listening Skills . . . Speaking Skills . . . Grammar   Skills . . . Writing Skills . . . Reading Skills . . . Library Skills . . . Spelling Skills.

Advantages of the Open-Space School Design . . . Renovations of Conventional Plants to Create Open Space . . . Attitudinal Problems and How to Deal With Them . . . How an Individualized Program Can Be Implemented in a Conventional Setting.

The Role of the Media Specialist in Curriculum Development . . . The Role of the Media Specialist in the Implementation of the Discipline Areas . . . The Instructional Role of the Media Specialist in Proper Use of Library Skills . . . Learning Center—An Extension of the Media Services . . . Scheduling of Library Classes.

The Case for Mainstreaming . . . Alternative to the "Caste" System of Special Education . . . Procedural

Steps Toward Mainstreaming . . . Incorporating Special
Education Teachers into the Mainstream.

SETTING THE STAGE FOR EFFECTIVE SYSTEMATIC CHANGE

Technological, scientific, and social changes are taking place in the world at an unprecedented rate. The rate of change has accelerated to the point that it is difficult even for the specialist to keep up with what is happening in his own field. With the present geometric progression of knowledge, population, technology, and social change, stability has become a thing of the past and man's inability to cope has caused much frustration. Until man learns to adapt to a more volatile society these frustrations will continue. Herein lie the imperatives for the educational institutions within this society.

Traditionally, educational institutions have been slow to change, but as the demands of a rapidly changing society continue to make an impact on education, ripples are being made which are the prelude to major changes that will be forthcoming in education during the next two decades. Educational leaders will have not only an opportunity, but also a grave responsibility in shaping the future.

Today's children should be educated to live in a society that probably does not yet exist and they should be prepared for careers that are yet unknown. As educational leaders begin to internalize the implications for education, the necessary changes will become a reality. That time is upon us. As these changes begin to materialize in the schools of this nation, not only parents, but the entire civic community must be aware of the reasoning behind the anticipated changes. To alert the parents and the community of the coming changes and the reasons for them will be a part of your responsibility as an educational leader.

Who is responsible for creating conditions whereby the changes will become a reality? The responsibility rests with every individual, but traditionally only a small percentage of the population provides the leadership. This minority group of educational leaders will be referred to as change agents in the remainder of this book. All educational administrators will of necessity become change agents, but the change agent's role will not be limited to administrators. Students, parents, civic groups, teachers, and other professional groups will have a role to play, but this book is primarily concerned with the role of the educational administrator. Without their in-depth understanding of the problem, needed changes will not occur.

Characteristics of a Change Agent

A change agent, henceforth, will be defined as one who causes change to occur. This role, in the field of education, will be exciting and dynamic but not without risk. The change agent must be adventuresome, courageous, knowledgeable, perceptive, and willing to challenge the status quo. Let us assume that you are the change agent in your community. You must realize that changes take place in the minds of men when their thought processes are challenged. This process will remove you from the protective shadow of tradition and you will open yourself to attack from your critics. Your ability to perceive problems in advance and take steps to contravene them will greatly enhance your success rate. Therefore, it is important that you consider all of the ramifications involved as you approach the task of challenging established tradition in one of the oldest institutions in our society—education. As you proceed you must recognize and inspire the leadership abilities of others, for the job before you will require the creative talents of all concerned. Flexibility will be required of you, for there will be times when you need to operate at varying points along the continuum of leadership styles from the autocratic end to the democratic end, depending upon the circumstances. You should be willing to acknowledge error in judgment and be prepared to alter your course, though you should never lose sight of your end goal.

You must be prepared to have your own thoughts challenged, for they surely will be. Your ability to respond to the challenge will mean the difference between success and failure. You will not be able to avoid controversy for by your very nature you will be controversial. Many of the controversial problems with which you will have to deal will require political considerations or they will have political overtones and you must recognize this as a reality. Your timing will be an important factor and your ability to sense the proper timing will be helpful.

Although you should be knowledgeable in educational theory, you will have to be a realistic practitioner, for you will be expected to transform theoretical ideas into workable realities. It will not be necessary that you have all the answers in advance, but you must be able to raise legitimate questions, for in so doing you set the stage for effective, systematic change.

Essential Steps for Systematic Change

Since you will be controversial and the decisions that you render will often be controversial, you should clearly visualize what you hope to accomplish, establish your general objectives, and develop a plan of action to provide systematic direction to your efforts. Operating without such a plan will increase your vulnerability and impede your chance for success. This plan should be tailored to the unique needs of your school or school district. Many potentially great ideas have failed to materialize in the absence of the direction provided by a definitive plan.

Can you imagine a contractor constructing a nuclear power plant to generate electricity without a specific plan outlining every detail? Such an endeavor would be catastrophic and the results would be disastrous. So it is with implementing innovative concepts in education where you have to challenge decades of tradition. Concrete plans must be made which will enable you to accomplish your desired goal. This means that you must have some idea where you are going and a plan of action for getting there.

On the next few pages of this chapter the plan will be outlined which provided the needed direction for West Elementary School in which I serve as principal. West Elementary is located in a relatively small town in North Alabama with a population of approximately 15,000. The town is presently in transition from an agriculturally oriented community to an industrialized one. West Elementary is the newest of the two public elementary schools. The school was constructed on the west side of town in the early fifties in a low socio-economic area. Since its original construction there have been three additions to the school plant as it has grown over the past twenty-odd years. The student population, too, has changed as the school district now covers all socio-economic levels.

The school is adequately funded through the minimum program at the state level with the City of Cullman providing 15 percent of the operational funds. This is considered to be rather high for most cities of this size in Alabama and is indicative of the pride the citizens of Cullman take in their school system. One result of this innate pride is the fact that our school was among the first in Alabama to be accredited by the Southern Association and by the State Department of Education.

The excerpt shown in Figure 1-1, taken from the latest accreditation study shows the educational level of the community.

FIGURE 1-1: Educational Level of Parents
in the Community

Percentage of parents who did not
complete high school 34.9%
Percentage of parents who completed high
school but were not graduated from college...50.7%
Percentage of parents who were graduated
with AB or BS degree 9.2%
Percentage of parents with advanced degrees ..5.2%

While it is important that you know your community well, this will not be a deciding factor in the success of your endeavor. Your success will be much more dependent upon the attitude of those responsible for implementing effective change. The plan presented in this chapter can be altered to fit the unique needs of your community whether it is rural, urban, or the ghetto, for it deals with the specific needs of individual children regardless of their economic background.

One of the first steps is to clearly establish the direction in which you want to move and outline the general objectives that you hope to accomplish. Much thought, planning, and discussion among school personnel will be needed prior to making a public announcement of the direction in which you plan to move. A memo such as the one in Figure 1-2, which was used in our school, could be used to publicly announce your intentions and to help begin a campaign which will involve your parents in an intensive public relations effort. This public relations effort should help to inform parents of the suggested changes and to solicit their ideas and opinions.

FIGURE 1-2: Directions for the Future

MEMO

TO: PARENTS
FROM: THE PRINCIPAL
RE: DIRECTIONS FOR THE FUTURE

In light of the astronomical changes that are taking place in the world today, educational institutions must change or they will cease to exist as a viable institution in our society. With the rapid advancement of science and technology, we have seen man travel to and from the moon almost routinely. Medical science has eradicated many dread diseases, successfully transplanted the human heart, and is on the verge of actually creating life in the test tube. We are being told that the current body of knowledge is multiplying at an astronomical rate and this is just the beginning of things yet to come.Through scientific development man has created the means of destroying life on earth, or, if it is intelligently used, could provide the means for solving many of the world's problems. In spite of the unprecedented scientific and technological advances, man is faced with the most serious problems of all times which, if unchecked, could endanger his survival. The primary reason for this dilemma is that the advances in the scientific world have far outstripped the advances in the social realm, thereby creating a chasm which could prove detrimental to mankind unless he finds a way to bridge the gap between the two. How does this relate to education, or what are the implictions for education?

Many changes must be realized in the field of education before this gap is narrowed. Our educational system is rapidly becoming outdated, for it is not keeping pace with the other institutions within this society. Therefore, we are announcing that immediate steps will be taken to make West Elementary School a more viable institution. For too long our schools have demanded conformity rather than creativity. Schools are stifling initiative rather than promoting self-direction. Self-direction is the key to man's survival; therefore, we will set that as our major goal.

As we move in this direction we will shift emphasis from memory to inquiry, from a group-centered approach to an individual approach, from a teacher-centered curriculum to a child-centered curriculum, for we believe that changes of this nature will be needed if we expect to produce self-directed citizens. As we move to bring about these basic changes many things will need attention; many of the things we are doing in education will be challenged, and many things will be changed.

As to how we will achieve this broadly stated objective we are not sure, but we are sure that what we have done in the past is not the answer. As we issue this challenge we ask not for your blind support, but we ask that you join with us as we collectively seek solutions that will be needed in the future. We promise no miracles, no easy and immediate solutions to our problems, for they are long-range in nature and very complex, but we do pledge to you our very best.

To provide systematic direction, a plan of action should be developed by the staff in your school or school system. The plan should outline the key areas of concern to which you must ultimately address yourself as you prepare to move. The key areas of concern listed in Figure 1-3 provided the outline for a plan of action upon which we concentrated attention for several years. You will notice that we moved on several fronts simultaneously.

FIGURE 1-3: Plan of Action

I. Attitude
   A. Administrators
   B. Students

    C. Parents
    D. Teachers
  II. Curriculum Changes
    A. Basic Skills
    B. Basic Social Program
 III. Renovation of School Plant
    A. Development of Team Centers
    B. Development of Learning Centers
  IV. Staffing Patterns
   V. Evaluation and Reporting of Pupil Progress

In our school a status report was written on each of the areas of concern identified and presented to the Board of Education along with projections for the future. Once our plans received approval from the Board of Education the operation was officially underway. The procedures utilized in implementing our plan of action will be discussed in depth in subsequent chapters.

Identification and Utilization of Vital Forces Within the School and Community

As you begin to implement your plan of action you must recognize the potential risk involved. You should familiarize yourself with all of the forces in and around the school and community. Identification of these forces will enhance your ability to deal with potential problems. Among those things with which you should be familiar are the local power structure in the community, the various religious factions and their values, special interest cliques, civic clubs, as well as other political and nonpolitical forces. You must also be aware of the attitudes and values of school board members, fellow administrators, teachers, parents, and students.

The power structure of a community is a potential force with which you will need to be completely familiar. Though you will not necessarily need to control it or be a part of it, you should be keenly aware of its existence and its influence on matters relating to education.

The various religious factions within the community are often diverse and their impact upon education should not be discounted. The values held by different groups could be a potential factor as you challenge traditional concepts and you should be aware of your standing in relation to the different groups within the community.

There will be other special interest groups such as local civic clubs who may want to involve the school with their projects. You should be aware of their concerns and develop policies to govern that type of involvement. It is not important whether or not these activities relate to the changes that you might wish to implement. But if these groups are alienated because you have no systematic policy to govern such activities, you will have difficulty getting their support in time of need.

It is also important that you be aware of how fellow administrators, teachers, parents, and board members feel about what you wish to accomplish. These people will have direct or indirect impact in the community and this can affect your efforts. You do not necessarily have to agree with them but you do need to know where you stand and know upon whose support you can depend.

Though these kinds of things may appear to be insignificant and often they may not relate directly to what you are doing, you should be fully aware of forces of this nature. If you are ever pressed into a political confrontation, these little things become important.

I recall an incident which happened after the innovative concepts had been in operation for three years in our school. We had just begun to move the operation into the other schools in our system when a challenge came out of "left field" from a small group of five politically powerful parents (later known as The Committee of Five) who struck like a tornado and threw us into a major controversy for an entire year. These parents were not in the West Elementary School district and had not been involved in the public relations effort which was conducted for the parents of West Elementary

School; therefore, they did not fully comprehend what was happening.

They based their claim that the programs were not working upon one set of California Achievement Test scores which was released by the Education Study Commission. The scores during that year dropped slightly. The drop was not statistically significant, but it was used to serve their purpose. They carried their challenge before the Board of Education and demanded an investigation. Because of the political power that this group of five parents exercised in the community, the Board agreed to the investigation. Following one of the most extensive investigations of this nature ever conducted in our system, the Board voted unanimously to continue in the direction we were moving.

The challenge was leveled primarily at school administrators because "The Committee of Five" apparently wanted to get teacher support for their position. During the investigation which involved the State Department of Education, the Board found almost unanimous support of the program among teachers who were working in the programs. They also found overwhelming support in favor of the programs among the West Elementary School's parents and a majority support among parents in the entire community.

Had we not taken the time to cultivate parental support and had we not informed parents about what we were doing and the reasons for it, we would not have survived the onslaught. However, because of the grassroots support that we developed in the early stages, the entire concept survived and was strengthened as a result of the challenge.

In order to be completely fair to the "Committee of Five," however, we must acknowledge that they did cause some changes to take place which improved the overall operation, and we grew professionally from the controversy. It forced members of the Board of Education to delve into and find out what was happening in the system, whereas they had previously operated on blind faith. When they realized what was actually happening, it caused them to give greater support to the idea. It focused attention on the need for involving parents and keeping them informed about that which was happening in their schools.

Potential Problem Areas
of Which You Should Be Aware

Many millions of dollars have been spent on construction of fabulous school plants with beautiful open space. These are a dream to some educators, but are the source of much concern and frustration to others. Constructing the open-space school without giving adequate consideration to curriculum design, staffing patterns, or the attitudes of all concerned could create problems. You must decide upon your major areas of concern as you develop your plan of action and move on several fronts simultaneously.

Another potential problem is failure to build grassroots support among parents, teachers, civic groups, students, and other groups. If an idea or a concept is dependent upon one individual, it will have little depth. You should begin to build a broad base of support as rapidly as you can.

Failure to clearly define the purpose of the proposed changes and make provisions to evaluate can lead to severe problems. For example, if you concentrate your efforts in the affective domain and attempt to measure your success by use of achievement tests, you will encounter problems. If these kinds of things are not spelled out in advance, you will be hard pressed to explain them as an afterthought.

Your credibility is most important and you should take steps to keep parents completely informed. Never fail to level with parents or you will lose credibility and this will render you ineffective as a change agent. You will be allowed to make mistakes if you are able to admit them and change your direction.

Summary

It is urgent that parents be aware of the need for change in public education. As you prepare to bring about fun-

damental changes you should be keenly aware of the vital
forces operating within the community and keep them in
mind as you develop and implement your plan of action.
Such forces can be put to work for or against you. The direction they will take will depend in part upon your perception
of them and the way you deal with them. You must be aware
of the realities and recognize that there are political considerations that may influence your actions.

You should not leave yourself without alternatives.
These alternatives, however, should lead toward your overall
objectives.

Since you have realized the need for change and you
have a desire to challenge the status quo, you are in a position
to make a significant contribution to education. Though such
an effort will require much work, the rewards of bringing
about effective change will be great.

WINNING PARENTAL
SUPPORT

There exists within the milieu of our present culture a highly sophisticated and informed public which is beginning to scrutinize the motives of government, labor, industry, education, as well as other institutions within this society. The trend has manifested itself in the form of accountability. Accountability is increasingly being demanded of educational officials throughout the nation. As this demand increases, your credibility will be your greatest asset. Failure to recognize this reality could create unnecessary problems and seriously affect your chances for success. This credibility, or trustworthiness, can be earned through parental involvement and an absolute determination on your part to be completely candid with parents.

Parental Involvement

There are two major reasons why parents should be involved in the change process. First, parents must be kept fully informed of your goals and objectives and the underlying reasons for them. Secondly, you will need to establish a systematic vehicle whereby you can work to modify parental attitude.

Parental involvement is paramount in gaining parental acceptance. When parents realize the need, and understand the reasons, for change, they will accept it and support it. No one readily accepts those things which they do not understand.

This was clearly illustrated during the initial stages of our planning when the word spread in the community that we were going to "knock out all the walls" in the school and allow the children to "do their own thing" if and when they so desired. Some of the parents who had not attended the briefings for parents and did not fully comprehend what was going on suddenly became alarmed to the point that they started circulating a petition to stop the entire operation. They started calling board members, attending the parent seminars, and asking questions about what was happening. This provided an opportunity to get more parents involved, although there were times when I felt I was having to explain the operation entirely too much. However, as long as parents were concerned and raising questions, I felt I had a responsibility to respond. As a result of the intensive public relations effort which will be described in depth in the remainder of this chapter, we gradually eliminated the concerns of most of these parents. Of great help to us were the parents who had attended previous seminars and were informed as to what we were doing and the reasons for it. They helped to allay the concerns of the dissident parents as they spoke out in our support.

Immediately prior to the Board's final acceptance of our plan, we called an open meeting for all parents to express their views and raise any questions they desired. All members of the Board of Education were present. The dissident parents were present and when the floor was opened for questions, they dominated the session. As the meeting progressed it became evident that they were in a very small minority and the overwhelming majority supported the effort.

One gentleman demanded to know why the sudden changes were being pushed so vigorously when we were not sure of exactly where we were going. We explained that we had been laying the groundwork for about three years and that the time had come to move ahead. To our way of thinking, we had proceeded cautiously and slowly. The parents who had been involved were quick to defend this position, for they knew what had preceded this move which was to launch us on the way toward implementation of a completely individualized instructional program throughout the entire school. As the meeting ended it was very evident to the members of the Board of Education and to everyone in attendance that we had adequately laid the foundation and that the vocal opposition was, in fact, token opposition.

The Superintendent of Education, Dr. A. W. Dennis, gave strong support to the endeavor and upon his recommendation the Board of Education approved the proposal and encouraged us to move ahead.

If we had not involved the parents early in the initial stages, thereby winning their support, we would have been left wondering what we did wrong after the opposition "came out of the woodwork" and started sounding off so loudly.

There are any number of options available to you for involving parents. The options used in our school included:

1. Newsletters
2. Memorandums
3. Bulletins
4. PTA meetings
5. Parental Surveys
6. Parent Curriculum Guides

7. Parent Conferences

8. Parent Seminars

The memorandums, bulletins, PTA meetings, and newsletters were primarily used to communicate specific information to parents and, occasionally, to correct some of the misconceptions regarding what we were trying to accomplish. The parental surveys were designed to gather information regarding parental attitudes and to further involve them in the change process by seeking their ideas and opinions about specific issues. Through the use of parental surveys, we were able to spot potential areas of concern and this often provided us with time to take action before it evolved into a problem. The parental curriculum guide was later designed for the express purpose of helping parents better understand the curriculum innovations which were being developed and enabling them to track their child's progress throughout his tenure in that curriculum.

Seminars to Involve and Inform Parents

The parent seminar proved to be the most useful technique employed in our school for it provided for a two-way exchange of ideas and opinions. Such seminars provided the vehicle whereby we were able to modify or change parental attitude when we felt that it was needed. In addition, the seminars provided parents the opportunity for an open forum for any issue they wished to discuss.

In the initial stages of this project we organized a series of parent seminars to begin orienting parents regarding basic philosophy, goals, and objectives along with the underlying reasons. We also encouraged parents to share their concerns in order that we might be in a position to give adequate consideration to them. The size of the groups was kept to a minimum of twenty to thirty parents to insure participation in the discussions.

Once we were ready to proceed with the parental seminars, invitations were sent home by students. The major thrust of the memo in Figure 2-1 was the orientation of parents to the school's philosophy and an effort to begin building a background for a move toward individualized instruction.

The seminars usually started with a brief overview of what we wished to accomplish, and the underlying reasons. In the first series of seminars we focused attention upon one of our major areas of concern as identified in our plan of action—the evaluation and reporting of pupil progress. The detailed techniques utilized in this area of concern will be discussed in depth in Chapter Six. Such discussions were followed by a tour of the school plant to enable parents to observe first-hand what was happening in the classrooms. The sessions were usually ended with a question-and-answer session in which we encouraged parents to react to what they had seen and heard. This provided us with valuable information, for we were able to pinpoint specific areas of concern for future seminars.

For example, if we picked up the cue in the question-and-answer session that parents were concerned about how students would be motivated to work if grades were removed, we included that topic in the next seminar; or if parents were concerned about how we could individualize instruction with twenty-five to thirty students and one teacher, our future seminars went in that direction. By listening to underlying concerns you will be in a position to design your public relations program around that topic of concern and prevent a great deal of wild speculation on the part of some parents. It will also help you to deal with real concerns of parents.

We were always candid with parents and if we disagreed with them on an issue, we explained why we disagreed. We readily acknowledged that we did not have all the answers but that we would collectively seek the appropriate solutions. This candor proved to be advantageous, for it enhanced our credibility.

FIGURE 2-1: Parent Seminars

MEMO

TO: PARENTS
FROM: THE PRINCIPAL
RE: PARENT SEMINAR

All parents who have children in the fifth grade are invited to attend a parent seminar at school tomorrow from 9:30 until 12:00 noon. Coffee and doughnuts will be served and each of you will be invited to have lunch with us. See the agenda below:

Agenda for Parent Seminar

9:30 - 10:00—Overview of School Philosophy
10:00 - 10:30—Individualized Instruction
                        What
                        Why
                        Who
                        When
                        How
10:30 - 11:00—Evaluating and Reporting Pupil
                        Progress in an Individualized
                        Program
11:00 - 11:10—Break-coffee and doughnuts
11:00 - 11:45—Classroom Visitation and
                        Tour of School Plant
11:45 - 12:00—Question and Answer Session

When we found our position to be indefensible, we acknowledged it and moved to alter that position. We always kept our options open and usually had an alternate plan in reserve which led toward our end goal. The importance of building strong grassroots support with parents cannot be overstressed.

With adequate planning, hard work, and a sincere belief in people, coupled with a little old-fashioned honesty, you can achieve beyond your expectations.

Effective Use of Parental Surveys

An informal parental survey is a viable tool with which you can gather the kinds of data that will allow you to become knowledgeable of parental concerns, thereby enabling you to identify potential problems. There are two kinds of survey available to you depending upon the kind of information you are seeking:

1. Surveys designed to get parental thinking prior to making the change.

2. Surveys to determine the degree of support for a given idea or concept which has already been put into operation.

Both types of survey will serve an important function for you. The sample survey shown in Figure 2-2 was used to ascertain the degree of support for a few ideas with which we were concerned. This survey was conducted during the second year of the project. We needed the data to reinforce our position with the Board of Education as well as with skeptics on the staff who were in doubt about how parents were accepting an idea.

This parental survey was designed to check on parental attitudes concerning several key items which had already been implemented. It provided us with valuable information and helped us to determine what, if anything, we needed to do concerning those items. It provided us with positive information that reinforced our position on several key items.

We always tabulated the results of such surveys and made it available to our parents. This technique helped to further strengthen our position with skeptical parents and teachers, as well as members of the Board of Education. The memo shown in Figure 2-3 was used to report the results to parents.

FIGURE 2-2: Parental Survey

MEMO

TO: PARENTS
FROM: THE PRINCIPAL
RE: PARENTAL SURVEY

Parents, you are one of one hundred randomly selected parents being asked to respond to this questionnaire. Please respond to the questions but do not sign your name. The data being collected will be used by school officials to evaluate our present position and to make further changes if warranted.

1. Have you attended a parent seminar this year?
2. If so, do you feel that it was worth your time?
3. Have you attended a parent-teacher conference this year?
4. Have these conferences provided you with the information you wanted?
5. Are you familiar with the Wisconsin Reading Design currently in use in our school?
6. Do you approve of the Wisconsin Reading Design?
7. Are you familiar with the Math program currently in use?
8. Do you approve of this Math program?
9. Do you feel that we should individualize our instructional program?
10. Please check one of the following, concerning reporting of pupil progress.
    a. I prefer parent-teacher conferences and narrative reports.
    b. I prefer a return to letter grades.
    c. I prefer narrative reports only.
    d. Other (Please specify)

FIGURE 2-3: Results of Parental Survey

MEMO

TO: PARENTS
FROM: THE PRINCIPAL
RE: RESULTS OF A PARENTAL SURVEY
            CONDUCTED LAST WEEK

    A few days ago one hundred randomly selected parents were asked to respond to a survey to provide feedback on how they felt about specific items of interest to school officials. The results have been tabulated as reported below:

1. Have you attended a parent seminar this year?
   44% No
   56% Yes

2. If so, do you feel that it was worth your time?
    3% No
   97% Yes

3. Have you attended a parent conference this year?
   100% Yes

4. Have these conferences provided you with the kinds of information you wanted?
    3% No
   97% Yes

5. Are you familiar with the Wisconsin Reading Design currently in use in our school?
   45% No
   39% Yes
   16% No response

6. Do you approve of the Wisconsin Reading Design?
    0% No
   45% Yes
   55% No response

7. Are you familiar with the Math Program currently in use?
   7% No
   93% Yes
8. Do you approve of the Math Program?
   10% No
   90% Yes
9. Do you feel that we should individualize our instructional program?
   2% No
   98% Yes
10. Please check one of the following, concerning reporting of pupil progress:
    50% I prefer parent-teacher conferences and narrative reports.
    12% I prefer a return to letter grades.
    25% I prefer narrative reports only.
    13% Other (This group wanted some other combination of narrative reports and parent-teacher conferences.)

After carefully analyzing the results of the above survey, we were in a position to make some decisions as to what we should do next. The following conclusions were drawn from the results of the survey.

Conclusion 1

After carefully studying the results of items seven and eight, it was decided that we no longer needed to concentrate an excessive amount of time on the Math Program. It appeared to be well understood and accepted by parents. As a result it was discussed only when questions were raised or in a new-parent seminar.

Conclusion 2

As a result of items five and six it was decided that more time should be spent on explaining the Wisconsin Reading Design, for the parents were not very familiar with it. It should be noted that more supported it than were familiar with it, which indicated a high level of confidence in school officials.

Conclusion 3

It was also determined that parents were generally supportive of our efforts to eliminate letter grades, but there was less uniformity of agreement concerning the alternatives. This indicated to us that we needed to concentrate our efforts on developing the appropriate alternatives rather than trying to convince parents that letter grades were not sufficient.

Conclusion 4

It was concluded that the seminars were serving their objectives based upon items one and two.

Conclusion 5

It was also noted that those who called for a return to letter grades had not attended the parent seminar. Thus we concluded that the seminars were helpful in modifying parental attitude.

The parental survey can be of value to you in the following ways:

1. It can provide you with information to which you would not otherwise have access.

2. It will also help to enhance your credibility.

3. It will give direction to your efforts and enable you to zero in on the issues that are in greatest need from the parent's point of view.

4. It will provide you with information to counter the critics when they challenge an idea on the grounds that parents will not support an idea.

5. It will assure your parents that you care about what they feel is important.

Other Forms of Communication with Parents

The best public relations effort that any school could have is reflected through your students. If they are learning and are happy in school, this will be communicated to parents and it will be reflected in their attitudes toward the school.

Strong emphasis should be placed upon developing a pleasant school environment in which students are happy and enjoy school. This focuses attention upon the curriculum, for an individualized program will require curriculum changes.

The physical facilities are important to the school environment. A well-kept, clean, air-conditioned facility with carpet provides a much more pleasant atmosphere than the unkempt, dirty, run-down, drab, classroom which many students in this nation are forced to endure. Classrooms should be alive, well-kept, clean, and as comfortable as possible. Such conditions will make a tremendous difference in a student's morale, and his desire to work will be greatly enhanced in an atmosphere which is conducive to learning.

The non-professional staff in any school also plays an important role toward the operation of the entire program. A high morale among this group is as important as that of the professional staff. They serve an important function in the overall public relations program, for it is not unusual for parents to ask these people what their opinions are regarding school operations. Often times they are listened to as much as, if not more than, members of the professional staff.

It would be much better to have them respond in a positive way to a concerned parent than to have them take the attitude that those teachers have "lost their minds." They should be informed about the reasons behind the changes that you are attempting to bring about in order that they can respond positively to parents in the community. Collectively, all of these kinds of apparently insignificant details can make a big difference.

Summary

The credibility of a change agent is vital, especially at a time when the motives of almost every institution are being challenged. The implications for the educational administrator are evident. You must take steps to insure a high degree of credibility. This can be achieved through parental involvement and a determination on your part to be completely candid with parents.

Parents can be involved in many ways through the use of parent seminars, parent conferences, memos, newsletters, bulletins, parental surveys and PTA meetings. You should decide which techniques will serve you best and develop a systematic plan of action.

There are two basic reasons for this systematic parental involvement. First, you must keep parents fully informed of your objectives and the underlying reasoning. Secondly, you need to develop a vehicle whereby you can work to modify parental attitude. You should be prepared to explain your reasoning to parents should you disagree with them.

Finally, you should strive to develop a good learning environment, giving attention to small detail. You must develop an instructional program in which every child can achieve success, for if the child is learning, he will reflect more positive attitudes and parents will respond accordingly.

CHANGING FACULTY ATTITUDES—
A CRITICAL FUNCTION

The teacher's relationship with the student is the single most important factor in the learning process. It stands to reason that his or her perception of children and how they learn is the fundamental key to positive change. It is also an accepted reality that no improvements are going to result without change. Therefore, before educators change their way of thinking about children or before such changes are reflected in the teaching-learning process, attitudes must be modified or changed.

Though it is possible for a forced change in behavior to result in changed attitudes, it is more desirable that attitudinal change precede behavioral change. Changing attitudes is important in any viable institution, but is especially crucial in education.

Success Is an Attitude

It has been said that success is about ninety percent attitude and ten percent ability. If you accept this premise, the implications for you as a change agent are evident. Your major responsibility will be to make a concentrated effort to improve, change, or modify staff attitude. In any give staff you will find diverse opinion regarding the organization and implementation of the instructional program. There is little uniformity among educators concerning the primary objectives of education and even less uniformity on how these objectives should be accomplished.

In recent years another dimension, collective bargaining, has brought about a polarization of attitudes between administrators and teachers. This movement has given rise to a new breed of teachers and administrators with each grappling for power in decision-making. Both teachers and administrators must realize that the ultimate answer lies in the development of a "true team spirit" in which administrators and teachers work cooperatively in a completely open and honest atmosphere. In the absence of this "team spirit" attitudes will continue to polarize.

As an administrator you must work to improve attitudes of all concerned. You must recognize that teachers should be involved in the decision-making process, not because they demand it, but because better decisions will result when the creative minds of all educators are focused upon the problems. Teachers do not want nor will they accept the paternalistic overtures of the past, but they do want and deserve complete candor. At the same time teachers must realize that if the educational institution is to remain a viable one which will be responsive to the needs of an ever-changing society, then someone must assume the responsibility for making administrative decisions that are necessary for the daily operation of the schools. Therefore, the major question to which you must address yourself is—how can I, as an administrator, challenge the prevailing attitude and at the same time involve teachers in the process?

Using the School Philosophy to Provide Direction

Since there are so many diverse ideas regarding the education of the whole child, it is necessary that a school philosophy be developed and used to provide systematic direction to your efforts. Parents, teachers, and administrators should be involved in the development of the school philosophy. Once the philosophy has been established or agreed upon, then total support should be expected. The philosophy will be used to give direction to the total school program and will provide guidelines upon which you can base your challenge of the status quo.

To challenge a teaching method or a technique without rhyme or reason may alienate attitudes, thus closing channels of communication. If, however, the challenge is rooted in the accepted philosophy, you will *open* channels of communication and alternatives can be considered. The following statement of philosophy provided guidance and the basis for the challenge in our school as we were involved in the change process. (See Figure 3-1.)

Once a consensus of opinion was reached regarding the school philosophy, it was formally adopted and served as the basis for many challenges that were yet to come concerning what was taking place in the classroom. This philosophy was used to point out the conflicts between that which we claimed to believe and that which was actually taking place in the classroom. As these challenges were leveled, controversy often erupted. This controversy served to focus attention upon the issue. At this point attitudes had already begun to undergo change. The following memo is one example of how the philosophy was used as a basis for challenging a common practice which was in conflict with the philosophy. (See Figure 3-2.)

FIGURE 3-1: School Philosophy

Our school is an institution of the community which created it and supports it; therefore, we are of the opinion that it should serve the needs of the community. This institution should be responsive to the concerns of the community and at the same time move forward. It must be flexible enough to respond to the changing needs of the community, yet stable enough to serve as a unifying force in a volatile society. It must change rapidly from an institution which imparts factual information to one which promotes self-direction.

We believe that neither parents, administrators, nor teachers educate students, but they are all instrumental in structuring the environment which will allow the child to educate himself.

We further believe that every individual is ultimately responsible for his own education. It should be remembered that one's education results from his interaction with his environment and we, as parents and educators, serve only to structure controlled situations within that environment which will be conducive to learning. The actual learning results directly from the child's conception or his internalization of a given set of circumstances; therefore, the learning process is unique for each individual. Until parents, teachers, and administrators internalize this concept, the educational process will be reduced to mere indoctrination and self-direction will be stifled.

We recognize and accept our responsibility for structuring this learning environment. A vital part of this is reflected every time a decision is made concerning the materials to be used, the programs to be implemented, and textbooks to be adopted, for all of these things are conducive to a good learning environment.

We do not believe that learning could or should be confined to the structured situations in the classroom. It is recognized that the world offers unlimited possibilities and most real learning probably takes place outside the classroom.

We further believe that the school must provide an instructional program that will meet the needs of each individual child. In order to do this we must move from a group-oriented approach to an individualized approach, from a graded school to a non-graded one, from emphasis on memory to emphasis on inquiry, and from emphasis on extrinsic motivation to emphasis on intrinsic motivation.

Our educational system must be grounded firmly in sound educational theory rather than upon such superficial devices as grades, failure or threat of failure, as well as many other extrinsic devices found to be prevalent in many schools across the nation.

FIGURE 3-2: Ability Grouping

MEMO

TO: TEACHERS
FROM: THE PRINCIPAL
RE: ABILITY GROUPING OF STUDENTS

Each of you is to be commended for your contribution to the recently approved school philosophy. This philosophy will serve as a guide to our efforts as we move to challenge the status quo. We should recognize that as this is done controversy will arise. Out of this controversy will come change and out of change will come improvement. If we will keep this in mind, we will be in a position to understand and cope with the controversy, for it will become an asset.

One common practice which is prevalent in this school system which is in conflict with our school philosophy is that of ability grouping. Since it contradicts our stated philosophy, it has no place among the organizational patterns in our system. This practice is hereby challenged based upon the following statements from our philosophy:

" . . .We further believe that the school must provide an instructional program that will meet the needs of each individual child . . . "
" . . . the school must move from a group-oriented approach to an individual approach . . . "

If we believe in an individualized approach to instruction as we indicated in our philosophy, then we need not be concerned with which group a child should be placed, rather our primary concern becomes that of diagnosing specific instructional needs and providing appropriate instruction to remedy that need. Any attempt to group away differences is not only impractical, it is impossible. We rationalize that ability grouping narrows the range and makes it easier to deal with individual differences. This, unfortunately, implies a false premise, for no matter what kind of grouping techniques one uses there will still be as

> many different needs within each group as there are
> individuals. This further implies that a group ap-
> proach is desirable, an idea that has been rejected in
> our philosophy.
>
> Further, if we really believe in ability grouping,
> we are in effect saying that differences in students
> should be discouraged, a philosophy with which I can-
> not agree. I therefore call upon you to begin consider-
> ing other alternatives for meeting the needs of our
> children.

Though this memo did not bring an immediate end to
the practice of ability grouping, it did serve to focus attention
on the issue. The ensuing discussions eventually led toward
the development of an individualized instructional program
in which ability grouping was no longer needed or desired.

Many such memos were used during the next few years
to challenge everything from traditional grading practices to
placing students in the halls for punishment. This proved to
be an effective method for getting teachers to think about
what they were doing in the classroom as it related to what
they said they believed. Once an individual begins thinking
about an idea, attitudes will change. This kind of approach
merely provided a forum for getting attention focused upon
the issue.

Other Effective Strategies
for Modifying Attitude

Another technique which was used in conjunction with
the one described above was the teacher survey of attitudes.
Following a brief period of discussion on the above topic of
ability grouping, a survey was conducted to determine how
the staff felt about the issue. (See Figure 3-3.)

FIGURE 3-3: Survey of Opinion

MEMO

TO: TEACHERS
FROM: THE PRINCIPAL
RE: SURVEY OF OPINION

In a recent memo the continued use of ability grouping as an alternative for grouping students for instruction was challenged, based upon the fact that it was in conflict with our philosophy. I would like to know your feelings concerning the matter. Please respond to the following survey.

1. Do you believe that ability grouping is in conflict with our written philosophy?
2. In your opinion does ability grouping make it easier for you to deal with individual needs of children?
3. Do you have any research which would indicate that ability grouping has effectively improved the learning of all students?
4. If better alternatives were presented to you, would you be receptive?
5. Do you accept the premise, as was discussed in a recent faculty meeting, that ability grouping sets up a type of caste system for the students?
6. Do you feel that a child should be placed in a group situation in which attention will be focused upon the fact that he is a slow learner?
7. Do you favor the immediate end to ability grouping?
8. Do you believe that ability grouping could be harmful to the self-concept of some children?
9. Do you feel that you are ever justified in setting up a situation which could be harmful to the child's self-concept?
10. Would you be willing to work with the slowest group?
11. Why do you favor or not favor ability grouping?

The results of such surveys were compiled and given to the staff. From this they could see that there were opposing views concerning the issue and this in itself caused teachers in many instances to reconsider their position. Through the use of surveys of this nature you can determine the prevailing attitudes and it will help you to more adequately time your move. For example, if you find that ninety percent of the teachers favored an immediate end to the practice of ability grouping, you could take steps to eliminate it almost immediately. However, if you found that only a small percentage of the teachers favored its immediate elimination, you would probably wish to spend additional time establishing a more solid foundation for this issue.

Surveys of this nature will be helpful to you in assessing prevailing attitudes regarding many of the issues you might wish to challenge. The results of these surveys were filed for future reference in the event that they were needed to document a given teacher's position concerning the matter. Once you understand how teachers feel about an issue and why they feel as they do, then you are in a position to observe their feelings objectively, and take steps to modify that position if you deem it necessary.

Another technique that was used occasionally was to move to an extreme position for purpose of debate, then compromise that extreme position, thus modifying attitudes.

One example where this technique was successfully used dealt with the issue of cross-age or cross-grade grouping of students. It was my desire to eliminate any pretense that differences in children could be grouped away and to create a situation that would cause teachers to seek alternative approaches to instruction.

My immediate objective was to group the first and second year students together and the third, fourth, and fifth year students together. I recognized that this break with tradition would cause a great deal of concern on the part of some teachers, therefore the memo illustrated in Figure 3-4 was used to present an extreme position to the teachers, a position upon which I was prepared to compromise and still achieve my objective.

FIGURE 3-4: Cross-Grade Grouping

MEMO

TO: TEACHERS
FROM: THE PRINCIPAL
RE: CROSS-GRADE GROUPING PROPOSAL

As each of you knows, we have committed ourselves to the development of a completely individualized instructional approach. If we concern ourselves with the specific needs of individuals, then the grouping patterns we use will make little difference. As we attempt to break with established tradition, it sometimes becomes necessary to create situations which will enable us, or cause us, to look for alternative procedures. We have aimed our instruction at the average student in a particular grade level, for we were concerned about meeting the needs of the majority of the students in a given class. However, as we move toward an individualized approach, the group will no longer be "the" important factor.

In order to create a situation which will cause us to look for alternatives in our instructional approach, I am recommending that we begin grouping students across grade lines.

I am proposing that we organize our homeroom groups across all five grade lines. This will mean that each team will have students from all five grades. This is a proposal only, but I would like for you to give serious consideration to it.

This memo brought a storm of protest, but it also caused teachers to begin considering alternatives. During the course of the debate which followed, the teachers agreed that we might be able to cross one or two grade lines but certainly not five, whereupon, I accepted the compromise and implemented my original objective to everyone's relief.

I had compromised my extreme position and agreed to accept the position of the teachers. While this technique may appear to be a little devious, I call it "stretching the imagination" in order to get people thinking. A word of caution,

however,—if this technique is over-used, it may lose its effectiveness.

Still another idea for modifying teacher attitude was to
force a change in behavior and wait for an attitude change.
Though this should not be used excessively, it will work in
some instances. You must realize that you will not get one-
hundred percent support for an idea one-hundred percent of
the time. Once you determine that you have the balance of
power in your favor, you can move to the autocratic end of the
continuum of leadership style and emphatically state your
position and move ahead. This technique was used as illustrated in the memo in Figure 3-5 when it became clear that
we would not be able to reach a consensus of opinion
regarding the matter of mainstreaming.

Though this idea met with strong resistance from a small
minority of teachers, it was strongly supported by the majority. As a result of this action, a much improved atmosphere was reached in which both parents and students no
longer objected to the services of the Special Resource
Teachers. Following a two- or three-year period, the teachers
who had been opposed to the idea accepted it more readily as
attitudes gradually changed after the issue had been forced
upon them.

Steps were taken to develop an up-to-date professional
library, and teachers were encouraged to read widely on the
non-graded, continuous progress, or individualized concept.
If and when the teachers held opposing views, they were encouraged to support their position with research.

Teachers were also encouraged to visit in other schools to
find out what was happening in other parts of the country.
They were given time off with all expenses paid to visit in
various schools or school systems. Many ideas were brought
back and incorporated into our total plan.

Such visitations need not be an expensive activity for the
school system. This is always an important factor during a
time when inflation is eating away at the education dollar
and school boards are faced with budget cuts.

FIGURE 3-5: Mainstreaming

MEMO

TO: TEACHERS
FROM: THE PRINCIPAL
RE: MAINSTREAMING OF SPECIAL
           EDUCATION STUDENTS

In light of recent discussions it has become evident that we will not be able to reach a consensus of opinion regarding the mainstreaming of our special education students; therefore, be informed that the following policy statement will become effective at the beginning of the next school year.

All special education students will be placed in the regular classroom. The Special Resource Teachers will serve in a tutorial capacity. All students identified as needing special instruction will be pulled from the regular classroom setting for specific instruction. They will participate in all activities in which the other students participate. All students will be involved in P.E. classes, homeroom activities, lunch, music, and in the basic social program. The special education students will be pulled out in small groups for skill instruction.

Further details will be passed on to you as soon as they are available. I would appreciate your cooperation in this matter. In my opinion, and in the opinion of the majority of this staff, this policy will improve the learning environment for all concerned.

Parent volunteers could be used in the classroom while teachers make their visitations. There is much to be learned in schools which are not far removed from your own. Teachers and principals will be able to pick up an idea here and there which can be applied in some way to give more strength to the program. Such trips can be provided for relatively little cost to the school system, yet valuable information can be realized.

Through the use of techniques of this nature, teacher attitude was gradually modified and professional growth took on new meaning. You should keep in mind that there are no teachers who do not wish to improve nor are there any who are not willing to change when they see the need for it. Therefore, your responsibility will be to help point out that need and help develop some techniques with which it can be done. The procedures discussed in this chapter worked in our situation.

The Changing Role of Teachers in a Team Approach

Another factor of which you should be aware is that once you begin to move toward an individualized approach in which you are seeking to promote self-direction on the part of the student, the roles of the student and teacher will be changed. If self-direction is to be promoted, students will need to assume more responsibility for their education. The basis in support of this is found in our school philosophy in the following statement:

" . . . We further believe that every individual is ultimately responsible for his own education . . ."

The teacher will move from the implied role that it is his or her responsibility to educate the student to that of helping to structure controlled situations which will cause the student to assume the initiative for his own learning. This can be accomplished through the development of curriculum materials as teachers work together in teams.

This was achieved in our school through the development of study guides in the areas of language arts and mathematics. A study guide is a package of not more than eight or ten pages of materials designed to help a student learn a given objective. The study guide will be described in depth in Chapter Eight. Through the use of diagnostic tests the teachers determine which study guides each student needs and assigns them to the student. At this point the activity becomes student directed, for the students are expected to begin working through the study guides. The teachers act as resource persons and move around the classroom giving individual attention to students needing it. If the students are able to proceed entirely on their own they do so. This frees the teachers to work with the students who need attention.

Working together in the team approach will allow teachers to complement the strengths of each other. For example, one teacher within a given team might place heavy emphasis on handwriting skills while another might not consider it very important. The two working together would probably maintain a good balance. Many weaknesses which were formerly covered in the self-contained classroom will become glaring and may cause some frustration and could be interpreted as weaknesses of the new approach. You should guard against allowing that to happen. After a year or two these frustrations will give way to the evolving "true team spirit" in which you will observe phenomenal professional growth. As this role changes, teacher attitude will be further modified and professional growth will take on new meaning. Teachers will become excited as they begin to assume the truly professional role that teachers rightly deserve. This will result in a renewed enthusiasm which will carry over to the students.

Utilizing Staff Leadership Potential

Though teacher attitude is a vital factor with which you must deal, it will also provide you with a wealth of leadership potential on which you will be able to draw. Once the direction has been determined and the wheels of change have been set in motion, you will need to take advantage of the creative talents at your command. The teachers will play a tremendous role in the field of public relations, hence they will be an important factor in helping to gain parental support. You will have no difficulty identifying the leaders for they will be open-minded individuals who are willing to venture out and try different approaches. They will not give excuses when an idea appears unworkable; rather they will offer alternatives. They will not be constant complainers but will remain very positive individuals. While they will not cling to tradition for the sake of tradition, they will challenge your thinking and your position on various issues from time to time. These are the kinds of people who should be placed in key positions within the team structure.

During the team planning sessions in which strategies are being considered, many ideas will be projected, some of which will offer solutions to problems and some of which will further aggravate the problems. For this reason it will be necessary that you develop some vehicle through which all ideas of all teachers can be aired, adequately considered, and utilized or rejected. Such ideas must be screened as to whether they are in conflict with the school philosophy and as to the degree that they might help to solve a problem. If they offer a possible solution and if they do not conflict with the school philosophy, then they should be considered. However, if they conflict with the school philosophy or if they will solve no problems, they should be rejected. This is where the team effort should be brought to bear on the problem, for if an idea is sound, it will stand the test and if it is unsound, it deserves to be questioned. In this team structure your leadership will emerge. It will also be shared for the leadership role will be changing depending upon the topic under discussion, the time, the place, and many other factors.

The details of how the team structure was organized in our school will be discussed in the following chapter. The "team spirit" that resulted was perhaps the source of greatest strength to the entire concept.

Summary

One of the most critical tasks facing you as a change agent will be that of changing or modifying staff attitude for it will be the key to your success. You will need to find a way to challenge the thoughts of teachers and at the same time involve them in the decision-making process. Both teachers and administrators must recognize and respect their particular roles and work cooperatively together. Teachers must be involved in decision-making, not because they demand it, but because better decisions will result.

There are many strategies through which prevailing attitudes may be challenged but you should have some basis for every challenge leveled. The school philosophy will provide the needed basis. Teachers, parents, and administrators should help to develop the school philosophy and once that is completed it will serve as a guide to your efforts.

ORGANIZATION OF TEAMS FOR EFFECTIVE MANAGEMENT

Cooperative decision-making is the key to developing a true team spirit which is the most desirable approach to curriculum planning and development. There are several distinct advantages of such an approach, but the most important one is that people generally give more enthusiastic support to decisions they help make. Before this team spirit emerges in its true form, you as an administrator, must be willing to share the decision-making role. This means involving teachers in the process. The team approach far exceeds the process used in team teaching, although team teaching is a vital part of the process.

The Advantages of a Team Approach

Educators working and planning cooperatively can develop more viable instructional programs. Such a team effort provides the means whereby the strengths of teachers and administrators can be successfully utilized, thereby giving greater strength to the total effort. This united effort will provide both the expertise and the flexibility needed to deal with the diverse needs of every school system. More specifically the team approach will enable school officials to eliminate the boredom which is prevalent in some schools by adding a greater variety to each teacher's class. This concept will inject new life and enthusiasm into an otherwise lifeless school as teachers realize their efforts and aspirations are not doomed by the whims of administrators.

This team effort will preclude the need for a divisive power struggle between administrators and teachers. In such a struggle conditions usually have deteriorated to a level in which teachers are demanding a greater voice in the decision-making process. This militant attitude serves only to place teachers and administrators in adverse roles which ends in a divisive power struggle, thus blocking communications and destroying credibility on the part of both. The team approach, on the other hand, will bring about a cooperative venture in which administrators work harmoniously with teachers to improve the educational opportunities for students.

Such a venture will call for some vehicle whereby both the administrator and the teacher can fulfill their respective responsibilities. As a change agent, you must realize that by working in this cooperative relationship neither your authority nor your effectiveness as an educational leader will be diminished. To the contrary, it will cause you and your staff to rise to a more sophisticated level of leadership. It will involve teachers in jointly assuming the responsibility that has traditionally been yours as an administrator, thereby, giving added strength to the total team effort.

Effective Involvement of Teachers in Decision Making

If teachers are to be systematically involved in the decision-making process, some vehicle must be developed. Such a system will allow both teachers and administrators to

fulfill their respective responsibilities. When our school
started moving toward a team approach such a vehicle did
not exist. However, as we moved through the change process
a system did evolve.

The staff was organized into five instructional units or
teams. Each team selected its own team leader who
represented the views of that team on the Instructional Policy
Committee, which was organized for the expressed purpose of
systematically involving teachers in the decision-making
process within the school. The Instructional Policy Committee, hereafter referred to as the IPC, under the chairmanship
of the principal, made all decisions regarding the instructional process. It should be remembered that this IPC did not
exist when we first started moving toward an individualized
approach, rather it evolved as the process developed.

Figure 4-1 will illustrate the general patterns utilized for
the five instructional teams. These were altered slightly from
year to year depending on the need and available staff.

FIGURE 4-1: Team Organizational Chart

1 Team Leader
3 Regular Teachers
1 Teacher Aide

Approximately 100 students grouped on a cross-
graded basis. (Described in depth in Chapter Five)

In addition to the team leaders, the librarian was included as a member of the IPC since her duties spanned all
five instructional teams. We later added a representative of
the special resource team until they were incorporated into
the regular teams as described in Chapter Twelve.

As chairman of the IPC it was the responsibility of the
principal to prepare an agenda and chair all meetings. This
group met weekly in the principal's office. Each teacher
received a copy of the agenda on Monday of each week. This
provided enough time for each team to discuss the agenda in
a planning session prior to the meeting of the IPC which was
usually held on Wednesday morning from 7:30 to 8:30.

The excerpt taken from the teacher's handbook, illustrated in Figure 4-2, will give a more detailed account of the operational procedures of the IPC.

FIGURE 4-2: Procedures for IPC

Operational Procedures
for the
Instructional Policy Committee

The Board of Education is the recognized policy-making body of this school system. These policies are implemented through the Superintendent's office. Authority is delegated to the principals of the respective schools to implement Board policy.

Policies and procedures of each of the respective schools are developed and implemented within the school under the leadership of the principal.

The principal hereby delegates authority to interpret and implement Board policy to the IPC subject to the restrictions as described herein.

Official Members of the Instructional Policy Committee:

Principal
Librarian
The Five Team Leaders
One Special Resource Teacher

The IPC will operate under the chairmanship of the Principal. It will be the responsibility of the chairman to prepare the agenda for all meetings, call the committee into session as needed and conduct all meetings. Following each meeting the chairman will cause the minutes to be written and distributed to all members of the staff.

All other members of the IPC will represent the interests of their respective teams and take action on all items on the agenda. Each staff member will be free to express his/her opinion regarding any item on the agenda. However, once action is officially taken by the IPC, every staff member will be expected to give

full support to the decision. It will be the responsibility of the team leaders to see that the desires of
the IPC are implemented in good faith. Failure of any
staff member to carry out the wishes of the IPC will be
considered to be in violation of official school policy.

General Guidelines

The school has set a goal for itself and is moving ahead to develop an operational, non-graded instructional program. There are certain pre-conceived
ideas that must be overcome in order to reach that
goal. The following guidelines will provide direction to
the efforts of the IPC.

* Regular meeting times will be mutually agreed
  upon by the committee.
* All members of the professional staff will receive
  an agenda at least two days prior to the meeting.
* No decision will be made by the Instructional
  Policy Committee which conflicts with the written philosophy.
* All staff members are invited to attend any session of the IPC and participate in the discussions.
  However, if the matter under discussion needs to
  be brought to a vote, only the official members
  will vote.
* Team leaders should discuss all decisions with
  their respective teams and give the underlying
  thinking which prompted the decision.

Through the IPC, teachers were systematically involved
in the decision-making process. This involvement helped to
build a broad base of support and greatly enhanced the
credibility of administrators and teachers, thus improving
communications between the two.

The agenda as noted in Figure 4-3, taken from the files,
exemplifies the kind of activities with which the IPC took action. It should be noted that occasionally an item appeared
on the agenda which did not call for affirmative action since

the issue had already been decided at a higher level. When this occurred, no pretense was made that the group would decide the issue. It was pointed out that the item was on the agenda only for information or perhaps for determining implementation procedures.

FIGURE 4-3: IPC Meeting

Instructional Policy Committee Meeting
Wednesday, November 24—7:30 a.m.
Principal's Office
Agenda

   I. Determine the implementation procedures for the new SCIS science program. (Science Curriculum Improvement Study)
  II. Determine the date that the team leaders will give their quarterly progress reports and the nature of the report.
 III. Determine which team will spearhead the Freedoms Foundation Program, the tentative date for completion and the theme.
 IV. Consider possible changes in the implementation guide for the Individually Guided Math Program.
  V. Review and take action on the new Teachers' Handbook that was given out last week. If there is anything in the handbook with which you do not agree, now is the time to challenge it.

After the IPC met and acted on all items on the above agenda, the minutes were written and given to all staff members as indicated in Figure 4-4.

FIGURE 4-4: Minutes of IPC Meeting

   I. Determine the implementation procedures for the new SCIS science program. (Science Curriculum Improvement Study)
      It was decided that the use of the new science kits should be limited to two of the three upper elementary teams. This will insure enough materials

for all children rather than spreading them too thinly. The Serendipity Unit reported that since they had already made plans for science, they would be happy for the other two units to use the new kits. This was agreed upon by all concerned. It was further decided that the Americus Unit and the Explorer Unit would use the life science kits and the physical science kits alternately. The two lower elementary units had previously worked out a solution.

II.   Determine the date that the team leaders will give their quarterly progress reports and the nature of the reports.

It was decided that the reports should be given at the next meeting of the IPC. Each team should include any unique ideas, the grouping procedures being used in the unit, any problems that they might be experiencing and the strengths of their procedures.

The principal requested that the reports be presented in written form, as well as orally, in order that they might be filed for the record.

III.   Consider possible changes in the implementation guide for the Individually Guided Math Program.

In light of recent discussions with the middle school math teachers, the results of our item analysis of the achievement test results, and the concerns expressed by members of our own staff, we believe that it will be in the best interest of all concerned to place greater emphasis on the basic mathematical operations and perhaps less emphasis on the non-essential skills. Therefore, it has been decided that you may, if you choose, accept less than 80% mastery in the areas of time, money, and measurement and concentrate the extra time on the basic operations.

IV.   Review and take action on the new Teachers' Handbook that was given out last month. If there is anything in the Handbook with which

you do not agree, now is the time to challenge
it.

This item was tabled until the following week.

Though the IPC did not bring an immediate end to all of
the controversy, or solve all our problems, it did:

1. provide a forum whereby teachers were systematically
   involved in decision-making.

2. help to build broad grassroots support of the individualized concept among staff members.

3. open lines of communication among staff members.

4. cause teachers to recognize the complexities of ad-
   ministration.

5. assist further development of the "true team spirit."

Professional Growth Through Team Planning

The team approach provided an ideal opportunity for
improving professional growth among staff members. As
teachers were brought into the decision-making process and
began to jointly assume the responsibilities for decision-
making, professional growth took on a new dimension as
teachers realized their voices could make a difference. For example, when an issue came before the IPC, every teacher had
an equal voice through his team leader. As the decisions were
being considered, the teachers were expected to express their
points of view as strongly as they desired. However, when an
issue was decided, everyone was expected to give full support.
It created a situation whereby teachers were supporting or
opposing decisions of their peers rather then decisions of the
principal.

Team planning was another important factor which
provided an opportunity for further professional growth.

Each of the teams was provided with one-hour planning time during the school day. This common planning time for members of each of the five teams was made possible through scheduling the P.E. classes in such a way that all teachers of a given Instructional Team were free for cooperative planning. While this cooperative planning ultimately proved very advantageous, it caused much tension initially. Many of the teachers had no previous experience in cooperative planning and they found that it was a new and often frustrating experience. This frustration was often vented among members of a given team to the point that communications were blocked. Out of all this "give and take" a different and more healthy climate evolved and professional growth was further enhanced. However, this climate caused the principal, working through the IPC, to develop a set of guidelines under which the teams would operate. The excerpt in Figure 4-5 from the Teachers' Handbook will explain the suggested procedures that were outlined.

FIGURE 4-5: Operational Ground Rules

No team will be effective without adequate planning on the part of the team leader. As team leader it will be your responsibility to see that the team operates as a cohesive unit. Without daily planning by the team leader, the group will not function as a team, therefore, the following ground rules are hereby adopted by the IPC:

1. Go into every unit meeting with a definite plan of action.
2. Know what you wish to accomplish by preparing an agenda.
3. Each team must keep a log or minutes on all planning sessions.
4. Both the agenda and the minutes will be subject to monthly audit.
5. Though you should not dictate policy to other members of your team, you should assert leadership by:

—delegating responsibility.

—encouraging team members to generate new ideas.

—terminating discussion at a feasible point.

—completing items of discussion before discussing other issues.

—supporting the decisions of the IPC completely.

—clarifying all decisions to your team members.

—following the five basic steps in problem solving:

*Pinpoint the exact problem before seeking solutions.

*Identify the obstacles hindering solutions.

*Outline your alternatives.

*Choose the best alternative available.

*Make a concentrated effort to follow through with your plan of action.

The above items, if followed, will increase your efficiency as a team leader and will enhance your team's effectiveness immeasurably.

After applying these suggestions and developing more experience at team planning, many of the problems gradually faded away and gave rise to a higher level of professional growth.

Potential Problems With Staff Organization and Suggestions on How to Cope With Them

While team teaching is an important part of the team approach, potential problems could develop unless adequate care is taken in organizing the instructional teams. For example, who is responsible for these kinds of decisions? How do you decide which teachers will work together? How would you handle a situation where there may be personality clashes between two teachers?

The principal must assume the responsibility for

organizing the various instructional units since this is primarily an administrative function. However, the teachers' feelings should be considered as an important factor in making such placements. No administrator would want to place two teachers in the same instructional unit if he knew that there were personality clashes that would prevent their working together harmoniously. The greatest problem is knowing all of the variables in advance. The principal should make provisions to secure as much information as possible prior to making such placements. This kind of information might be secured through private conferences with each teacher. It could be obtained through a survey, but it must be a survey which will be held in strict confidence.

In organizing the instructional teams in our school, I talked with the teachers and also asked them to respond to a survey. The memo shown in Figure 4-6 served to help me gather the data I wanted before making the various assignments to the teams.

A survey of this nature can provide you with the information needed in making teacher assignments. No teacher should be forced to work with any teacher with whom they feel they cannot function. By gathering this kind of information you will be in a position to consider the feelings of the staff as you make the assignments.

There are, however, no guarantees that all of your problems will be solved no matter how thorough you are in making the placements. I recall one incident that happened about three months after the teachers had been working together in teams. One of the team leaders walked into my office and said, "To hell with it! I have had it! I can't get the members of my team to agree on anything! They are all bickering and do not appear to be pleased with anything. It is time you did something about the situation!"

FIGURE 4-6: Teacher Placement

MEMO

TO: TEACHERS
FROM: THE PRINCIPAL
RE: QUESTIONNAIRE FOR TEACHER
          PLACEMENT

As each of you is aware, we have made provisions to organize the entire staff into instructional teams. It has also been decided that the principal will, of necessity, assume the total responsibility for placing teachers into the respective teams. I need to be aware of any preferences that you might have, or of any other special concerns that you might hold at this time. I am, therefore, asking you to respond to the following questionnaire. Your candid response will be greatly appreciated. Each of you has an absolute assurance that all information will be held in absolute confidence and will be destroyed as soon as it has served its purpose.

1. Please list your first, second, and third choice of the teacher with whom you would prefer to work as a team member.
   First Choice _____
   Second Choice _____
   Third Choice _____
2. Are there any teachers with whom you would prefer not to work? If so, list them.
3. Are there any members of the staff with whom you would refuse to work if assigned? If so, list them.
4. Please specify which level you would prefer to work:
   (a) Upper level   (b) Lower level
5. Please list any other concerns or reservations that you might have in regard to the placement of teachers.

Though I was aware that the problem had been building up, I made no move to intervene until I was asked. The team leader and I agreed that we should call the group together in my office for extensive discussion. To guide the discussion I established three ground rules:

1. Everyone was expected to express himself as candidly as possible as to what they considered the problem to be, with no punches pulled.

2. Everyone was expected to listen to what the others were saying without comment, until it was their turn to talk.

3. Everyone was going to leave the session and make an effort to improve the environment in which they were working.

When they walked into my office you could feel the coolness among the group members and none of them were willing to express themselves, or if they did, they were very guarded until I asked a few direct questions and probed under the surface. Then ground rule two was tossed out the window as the four teachers simultaneously vocalized their feelings. After about ten minutes they started the kind of discussion I felt might be profitable as they found common areas of agreement. From this point, constructive discussions were begun as they started finding ways to resolve their differences.

I would mislead you if I said that they never had any more problems but they started learning that it was better to express themselves candidly than to let tensions build up to "critical mass." They started to communicate with each other as the team spirit gradually emerged.

You will probably have to experience problems of this nature when you first move into such a teaming operation no matter how thoroughly you select the team members, but you must realize that this is nothing more than a developmental stage through which many teachers must go before they can operate as a team. Professional growth will result from such encounters, of that there is no doubt.

Summary

A true team effort provides for cooperative management of a total instructional program. This process involves team teaching, but it goes one important step further in that it includes decision-making. Such an approach has several distinct advantages:

1. It involves teachers in the decision-making role in a systematic way.

2. It broadens the base of support for the entire concept.

3. It precludes the need for the current power struggle in decision-making.

4. It helps to build close cooperation between the teachers and administrators instead of placing them in adversary roles.

5. It makes the innovative ideas less dependent upon the change agent, thus in all probability extends the life of the idea.

Teachers are systematically involved in the decision-making process through the IPC which is a representative group. Through this policy committee, all teachers have representation and all teachers are free to question an idea or express any opinion they so desire until such time that the IPC makes a decision. At that point every teacher on the staff is expected to give full support to the decision regardless of his personal opinion.

ASSIGNING STUDENTS TO
INSTRUCTIONAL TEAMS

With the advent of more individualized instructional programs the grouping patterns utilized in the schools across the nation will cease to be a major point of concern for educators. However, from a purely managerial standpoint, it will always be necessary to group students in some manner. The important thing to remember is that during the period of transition from the traditional graded concept to the completely individualized concept, cross-grade or cross-age grouping may help to dispell some of the preconceived ideas to which so many parents and educators have become accustomed, and it can help to create a situation which will cause educators to look for alternative instructional approaches.

Assigning Students to Homeroom Groups

Traditionally, students have been assigned to homeroom groups according to their grade or year in school. At age six most youngsters in this country enter the first grade. With few exceptions they are placed in a first grade class where they remain for one year, after which they are promoted to the second grade where they remain another year. The process continues until they complete twelve years of school. This routine procedure has become so ingrained in American education that many parents and educators tend to equate one's academic level with the year in school. Herein lies the false premise upon which many schools operate. Only in recent years have educators begun to acknowledge that this is an impractical situation, for academic progress can no longer be equated with the year in school or with a given grade level.

In an effort to break away from the false premise that grade levels are synonymous with some predetermined academic level, the students in our school were grouped across the traditional grade lines. Figure 5-1 illustrates how students were assigned to the respective teams by the principal.

FIGURE 5-1: Student Assignments

The following specialized personnel
served all the teams:
1 P. E. Teacher
1 Music Teacher
1 Librarian
2 Special Resource Teachers
1 Speech Therapist

Lower Elementary Teams

Apollo Unit

4 Teachers
50 First Year Students
50 Second Year Students

Rocket Unit

4 Teachers
50 First Year Students
50 Second Year Students

Upper Elementary Teams

Explorer Unit

3 Teachers
25 Third Year Students

Serendipity Unit

4 Teachers
33 Third Year Students

25 Fourth Year Students   33 Fourth Year Students
25 Fifth Year Students   33 Fifth Year Students

Americus Unit

 4 Teachers
33 Third Year Students
33 Fourth Year Students
33 Fifth Year Students

The team leader was responsible for assigning the students to the various homeroom teachers within each of the respective teams. The excerpt in Figure 5-2, taken from the Teachers' Handbook, spells out the limitations of the team leaders in placing students in the various homeroom groups.

FIGURE 5-2: Placement of Students

It will be the responsibility of the principal to assign students to their respective units. The first and second year students will be assigned to the team leaders in the lower elementary teams, while the third, fourth and fifth year students will be assigned to the team leaders of the upper elementary units. Each of the team leaders will in turn assign the students to their homeroom groups subject to the following two conditions:

1. Each teacher within a given team must be assigned an equal number of students from each grade level within that team.

2. Students may not be assigned to homeroom groups based upon any semblance of ability or achievement grouping.

It is important that you understand the reasons behind the grouping technique to be used. To group students across grade lines just to be different is insufficient reason. There were several reasons why our staff chose to group students across grade lines.

1. To break away from the false premise that grade levels are synonymous with academic achievement.

2. To deliberately widen the achievement span to encourage teachers to seek alternative teaching strategies by making it impossible to even attempt to teach the entire group in the same way.

3. To create a setting whereby students of varying age groups naturally work together.

4. To facilitate peer-tutoring by placing students of varying age groups in the same room.

In addition to the above reasons, two important by-products resulted from the cross-grade grouping.

1. The cross-grade grouping proved advantageous to the teachers who had previously taught only first year students, for they now had only one-half their students who could not read at the beginning of the school year. This made it possible for more independent work for the second year students, while the teacher was working with the first year students.

2. The cross-grade grouping made it possible to reduce the professional staff by equalizing the class load.

The Basis for Forming Instructional Groups

It should be remembered that in a truly individualized and/or non-graded instructional program, your major concern is to determine the specific skill needs of each individual and provide instruction accordingly. When this goal is fully realized the grouping techniques will cease to be a matter of concern and students could theoretically be grouped according to the color of their hair if you so choose.

However, there are two generally accepted methods for grouping students for instruction in an individualized and/or non-graded program:

1. Students may be randomly grouped.
2. Students may be grouped according to skill needs.

RANDOM GROUPING

Of the two grouping methods, the random grouping of students more nearly exemplifies the true non-graded or continuous progress instructional program. Students may be randomly grouped across grade lines. Then it will be necessary that the teachers determine the skill need of each child and provide curriculum materials to allow the student to work on that skill. In this kind of curriculum every child in a given classroom could be working on a different skill. This requires a highly structured program in which teachers determine the skill need of the student through the use of diagnostic tests. Once programs have been developed and curriculum materials organized into some definite format, grouping will cease to be a major problem.

Programs were developed in our school which made it possible for teachers to determine the specific skill need in the areas of language arts and mathematics. Such a program will require a continuum of skills and diagnostic tests for each skill identified. Once the skill need has been determined, study guides will be needed to enable the student to proceed on that particular skill.

The monumental task of developing a study guide for every skill identified was accomplished during the summer months in which approximately eight teachers were employed with Title I monies and monies from the General Fund. Parent volunteers helped with the typing and assembling of the study guides. We embarked upon this endeavor without the promise of any additional monies over the regular funding. About the only thing we had going for us was a determination to make the idea work.

After struggling for approximately two years, we developed a Title III ESEA proposal to obtain additional funding. The proposal was funded in the amount of $52,000 the first year, $50,000 the second year, and $40,000 the third and final year. This enabled us to employ a full-time curriculum coordinator and to purchase an off-set press and the needed equipment to print the program. The curriculum coordinator continued to develop and refine the program along with the assistance of the regular teachers. The fourth year, the project was validated for national dissemination, and another $25,000 was awarded that we might implement this.

While the $52,000 grant during the first year was small, comparatively speaking, it was concentrated in one school and used in conjunction with regular funds, which gave us a tremendous boost during the developmental stages of the programs. This made it possible for continued development of programs which enabled us to use random grouping of students.

SKILL GROUPING

Grouping students according to skill needs also requires that you have a continuum of skills identified and diagnostic tests for determining which skill a given child will need. Cross-grade grouping was helpful in this kind of situation in order to get enough students with common skill needs to justify assigning a teacher to the group. Such groups must remain flexible and will last from one to two weeks depending upon the students and the skill which they are learning. It will require continuous regrouping of students as skill needs change. The Wisconsin Reading Design, as described in Chapter Nine, utilized this type approach until we were able to develop study guides for the program, which enabled the teachers to handle diverse skill needs within their own team areas without the constant reshuffling of students.

The major advantage of this approach is that it can be implemented without the study guides. Its major disadvantage is the continuous regrouping of students and the continuous movement of students as they progress from one skill group to another.

Examples of each of the above curriculums will be described in depth in Chapters Eight and Nine. Figure 5-3 is an excerpt from the Teachers' Handbook which illustrates the general grouping patterns used in each of the major discipline areas. These guidelines, developed by the Instructional Policy Committee, outline the parameters within which teachers of a given team were expected to operate.

FIGURE 5-3: Guidelines for Instructional Grouping

The following guidelines are hereby adopted by the IPC to give direction to the grouping techniques which will be permitted for instructional purposes.

Grouping for Math Instruction

Since the math curriculum has been reorganized to the point that it will lend itself to a completely individualized approach, it is strongly suggested that the homeroom groups be used for math instruction. Each homeroom teacher will be responsible for keeping records in the math program and making sure that each child moves reasonably well through the math program. Students may not be regrouped on a graded basis for math.

Grouping for Language Arts

Since we have not completed the reorganization of the language arts curriculum, you may group or regroup students as you so desire except for the Wisconsin Word Attack Skills. Students in the word attack skills will be grouped according to skill needs. However, you are strongly urged to work across grade lines when you feel that you can.

There will be no permanent achievement or ability grouping at any time.

Grouping for Social Studies

Teachers are free to regroup within teams as desired except for permanent achievement or ability grouping. Again, you are strongly urged to work across grade lines in social studies if you feel that you can.

Grouping for Science
    Same as in Social Studies

Cross-Age Grouping

Cross-age grouping is becoming a more common method of organizing students for instruction for two essential reasons. First, it is more economical, and second, it will cause teachers to seek alternate approaches to instruction, since traditional graded approaches will not work when you group students across grade lines. This kind of approach is gaining momentum as educators begin to concern themselves with specific needs of children. As long as educators are group oriented, cross-age grouping will hold little or no appeal, but as this trend is gradually being reversed, educators are looking for alternatives. Educational administrators will find that cross-age grouping can be more economical because class loads can be equally assigned. If one teacher unit per every twenty-five teacher units could be eliminated by equally dividing the students, a substantial saving could be realized. Though this was not our primary purpose for cross-age grouping, it proved a worthy by-product.

Interest Grouping

Interest grouping is a grouping technique whereby students are free to choose their group based upon some special interest. This grouping practice probably has little or no place in the basic skills program such as reading and math, but it may serve well in the areas of social studies, science, literature, and art. It has come into vogue in recent years and has given rise to the mini-units and mini-courses that are prevalent in many elementary, middle, and secondary schools across this nation. Through the use of mini-units or mini-courses, students can make some choices in what they wish to study. If students are intensely interested in a given subject, they can take a concentrated course on that topic. This allows for a greater variety to be built into a curriculum.

Mini-units or mini-courses are ideal at the middle school level, for they allow students an opportunity to do some exploratory study at a crucial time in their lives. While we have used this technique only sparingly at the elementary level, the middle school uses it rather extensively. It is one of the most popular phases of the middle school curriculum.

Ability Grouping

Ability grouping is one of the most controversial grouping techniques used in the past few decades. While proponents have hailed it as the innovation of the century, opponents have condemned it as the worst possible villain in education in recent decades. While I would lean toward the latter point of view, it should be acknowledged that both views are probably exaggerated. The concept will be examined at this time as it relates to the school philosophy.

Proponents have defended ability grouping as being one way to approach the individual needs of students, for it allows students with similar abilities to be grouped together for instruction. With this grouping technique the individual needs of the various groups can be dealt with much more easily. It is possible for the faster students to move ahead, while the slower students move at a less rapid pace.

However, ability grouping must be examined in light of the school philosophy. When this was done in our school it was found wanting in at least one important respect. Ability grouping is premised upon the fact that students should be taught as groups rather than as individuals. In an individualized approach you are primarily concerned with the specific needs of each individual rather than the group. No group of students with similar abilities will necessarily have the same skill needs, therefore, ability grouping is of little value in an individualized program.

Achievement Grouping

Another technique of grouping which has some potential in an individualized instructional program is that of achievement grouping, which has been discussed in a previous paragraph. Though it will require the development of skill continuums, diagnostic procedures and management systems, it can be implemented without extensive work in organizing curriculum materials. Such a technique would serve well during a period of transition from a group approach to an individual approach.

In this approach the needs of each child are identified through some diagnostic procedure and the students are placed in groups with other students who have similar needs. Grade levels cease to be a concern with this grouping technique, for the main concern becomes that skill which is needed. It does not matter whether $5 \times 9 = 45$ is a third grade, a fourth grade, or a fifth grade level skill. When it is determined that the student does not know the skill, it should be taught at the proper time, regardless of the present grade level.

Achievement grouping would need to be kept flexible with provisions for students to move from one group to the next as the skills are mastered lest it lapse into ability grouping. Constant mobility of students is necessary in this kind of situation, thus the management system should be well-organized to prevent frustrations and wasted time. Such a system will be described in Chapter Nine.

Summary

In any instructional situation students must be grouped in some manner. The most important thing to remember when developing the grouping techniques is the underlying reasoning. Whether you use achievement-grouping, ability-grouping, cross-grade or cross-age grouping, grade level grouping, interest grouping, or some combination thereof, the method should be firmly rooted in your school philosophy. As long as the methods do not conflict with the school philosophy, your reasoning is defensible.

PROCEDURES FOR IMPLEMENTING ALTERNATIVE REPORTING SYSTEMS

In the initial plan of action developed by our staff, we identified as one of our major areas of concern that of evaluating and reporting pupil progress. Since this was a vital area, in our opinion, we devoted a great deal of attention to the matter. We felt that it was necessary to find alternatives to traditional reporting practices since they were incompatible with the individualized approach to instruction. Challenging such established tradition causes much concern on the part of parents and teachers; therefore, it requires much time and effort. This chapter will be devoted to the techniques utilized in bringing about the necessary changes.

The Need for Alternative Reporting Systems

As the school systems throughout the nation move toward more personalized curriculums, attention is being focused upon the procedures and techniques being utilized for evaluating and reporting pupil progress to parents. Letter grades as used in the past are incompatible with the newer curriculum approaches. School administrators are beginning to realize that evaluating and reporting of pupil progress is more complex than previously supposed and are searching for alternative reporting procedures. As this search commences, a few teachers and parents may become overly concerned and it will be necessary to modify attitudes of parents and teachers who cling to tradition.

Modifying Teacher Attitude
Toward Evaluation and Reporting

As you begin to implement alternatives, you will be aware of the amount of time and effort that you will need to devote to this issue. There are any number of ways which will enable you to modify staff attitude toward the continued use of grades. Several techniques which proved helpful in our school will be discussed.

Knowing your staff's attitudes concerning grades will enable you to take the necessary steps to modify those attitudes.

There are three necessary steps that should be taken prior to the elimination of letter grades:

1. Clearly define the philosophical basis for eliminating grades.

2. State the reasons as clearly as possible in language the layman can readily understand.

3. Be prepared to offer appropriate alternatives.

If your staff agrees that alternatives are needed, the change can be made rapidly. However, if there are teachers on your staff who feel strongly that letter grades are needed, more of your time will be spent altering that attitude.

Continued use of grades might be challenged as a viable method of reporting pupil progress through the use of a carefully worded memorandum to teachers. The one used in our school (Figure 6-1) was written in such a way that teachers would become concerned about the issue. It caused them to focus attention on the issue and the ensuing dialogue caused teacher attitude to begin undergoing change.

This memorandum was followed by an inservice meeting at which time the issue was discussed at length by teachers as each of them was given an opportunity to express feelings openly. The ensuing dialogue caused attention to be focused upon the matter and later resulted in the total elimination of letter grades.

In order to determine how each teacher felt regarding the use of letter grades, an opinion survey was conducted. The survey as illustrated in Figure 6-2 was not scientific, but it provided the information needed.

FIGURE 6-1: Reporting Procedures

MEMO

TO: TEACHERS
FROM: THE PRINCIPAL
RE: CURRENT EVALUATION AND REPORTING PROCEDURES

I would like to take this opportunity to express my appreciation to each of you for the hospitality you have demonstrated since I have been here. I am looking forward to working with each of you this school year.

Our major objective during this school year will be to bring about desirable change. It is my intention to take a very aggressive lead rather than to passively follow the lead of others. In my opinion, we must move ahead at an even more rapid pace than we have in the past.

We must remember that as we move out we are not always going to enjoy a tranquil atmosphere, for change does not take place in such an atmosphere. What we do will be controversial, for the status quo will be challenged. I will not hesitate to challenge any action that I feel is in conflict with our written philosophy.

Today I would like to challenge one issue that, in my opinion, is in direct violation of our stated philosophy. We are moving toward the development of a completely individualized instructional program. Traditional letter grades are not compatible with our present philosophy, a philosophy to which you recently subscribed.

In a graded instructional program where standards are predetermined, grades might give some indication as to the degree of attainment, but in a nongraded instructional program standards are set which are commensurate with the needs and abilities of the individual, therefore, grades can no longer serve a useful role and should be eliminated as soon as possible.

FIGURE 6-2: Opinion Survey

MEMO

TO: TEACHERS
FROM: THE PRINCIPAL
RE: OPINION SURVEY

Teachers, as a follow-up on our inservice session last Monday, I would appreciate your reaction to the questions below concerning the use of letter grades as a means of reporting pupil progress.

Yes No

__ __ 1. Do you favor the continued use of letter grades?

__ __ 2. Do you feel that letter grades help to motivate students to work?

__ __ 3. Do you feel that a child's grade should be based upon his ability?

__ __ 4. Do you feel that grades you give to children reflect only academic progress?

__ __ 5. Should grades reflect only academic progress?

6. What are some of the alternatives that you would propose?

Surveys of this nature were used to provide the information needed for future discussions in which specific points given in support of grades were challenged. Point by point most of the arguments given in support of grades gradually diminished, though a few persisted and were dealt with in the following way:

Each teacher was given the background data on three students (Figure 6-3) and was asked to assign a grade based on the data presented.

FIGURE 6-3: Data on Three Students

Jim
Age: 10
Grade: 5

Jim was a very articulate child who could express himself well orally but had some difficulty expressing himself on paper. His I.Q. was 98 and most of his teachers considered him to be a good, average student.

He became ill and missed three weeks of school during a given six week period and was unable to keep up his work. His parents tried to help him at home, but they were unable to teach all that was needed. On the tests that he had taken prior to his illness he made the following grades: 80, 90, and 85. After he became ill and was unable to attend regularly, his grades dropped to 50, 45, and 64, with a 58 on his six-weeks test.

Based upon this information, assign Jim a grade for the six-week period.

Jane

Age: 10

Grade: 5

Jane was a very bright girl with an I.Q. of 120 according to a recent test. She was a very capable student but had developed the idea that she did not need to study to make good grades. Her mother was very involved in various social clubs and did not spend as much time with Jane as she should have. Her father was an accomplished attorney and spent very little time with Jane and felt that PTAs were for women who had nothing else to do.

During a given reporting period, Jane made the following grades in math: 100, 100, 85, 95, 54, and 69. The teacher wrote a note to Jane's parents concerning the declining grades, to which the father responded implying that it was the teacher's responsibility to see that Jane kept her school work up to acceptable standards. However, he did talk to Jane and threatened to cut off her allowance unless she did better. Under this pressure, Jane copied a friend's test paper on the six-week test. When the teacher confronted her about the matter she first denied it but later admitted that she did copy for fear of losing her allowance.

What grade would you give Jane based upon the information above?

Tony
Age: 11
Grade: 5

Tony was a small, immature child whose I.Q. was only 77 according to a recent test. He was a lovable boy whose parents were in the lower socio-economic level. His father had been crippled for the past ten years and his mother worked as a maid at a local motel. Her work required that she stay late at night and Tony's father prepared his evening meal. Tony was very conscientious with his school work and in the opinion of the teachers, put forth all the effort that he had. He did excellent work for a child of his ability. During a given reporting period he made the following grades on his tests: 56, 70, 60, 48, 45, 65, and 68.

What grade would you give Tony based upon the information above?

After the teachers had assigned grades to the students, the results were documented as noted in Figure 6-4.

FIGURE 6-4: Summary of Grades

	A	B	C	D	F	I
Jim	0	1	8	14	1	1
Jane	0	6	7	6	5	1
Tony	3	4	10	3	5	0

Of the twenty-five teachers participating in this exercise we found that professional staff members were at odds over grades even when using the same data. For example, three teachers had indicated excellent progress for Tony while five teachers had declared him a failure. Six teachers indicated that Jane was a good student and five had declared her a failure.

In fact, the grades assigned by professional teachers who had access to the same data ranged from "A"s to "F"s because teachers had read their own values, feelings, background, and prejudices into the grades. As a result of our professional growth through the use of such activities, grades were replaced with parent-teacher conferences and narrative reports with ninety-five percent teacher support.

Effective Public Relation Ideas
to Win Parental Support

Although some of the procedures for modifying parental attitude were similar to those used with teachers, a slightly different approach was used. The major thrust of this effort was through parental seminars. Each parent was invited to attend a parent seminar as described in Chapter II. The groups were kept very small to insure the participation of all parents.

Each seminar was begun with a brief introduction of general activities of the school and a review on the direction in which the school was moving and the reasons for it. Letter grades, as a means of reporting pupil progress, were challenged and alternatives were projected. Following the remarks from school officials, a general discussion ensued concerning the validity of grades. All parents were encouraged to voice their feelings concerning the matter. During these discussions, mental notes were made concerning the potentially volatile issues so that future seminars could be organized to counter them or that they might be dealt with through the use of newsletters or memorandums to parents.

Following the discussion, the parents were given background data on three students and were asked to assign grades to each of them based upon the data given, just as the teachers had done. When the results were compiled and presented to them, they realized that grading students involved more than merely averaging a few test scores. This activity demonstrated that grades did, in fact, reflect more than pupil progress as parents realized how the values, background, and prejudices of teachers could become involved and confuse the issue. For all practical purposes, the argument that grades reflected actual pupil progress was found wanting and parental attitude began to change.

It was then pointed out that through parent-teacher conferences the same information could be conveyed to parents along with appropriate explanations and suggestions for improvement. Conferences would also provide the teachers with vitally needed information to which they might not otherwise have access.

The supposition that grades motivated students to work continued to hold validity for a few parents and teachers. They could not understand how students would work if grades were eliminated. This fallacy was dealt with through the use of letters, additional seminars, and memorandums. The memorandum in Figure 6-5 was typical of those used, not only to dispell the idea that students would not work without grades, but also to counter other related issues which arose.

The following year grades were replaced by a combination of narrative reports and parent-teacher conferences. A sample of the report card used for the narrative report is noted in Figure 6-6.

According to the surveys conducted during the following school year, it was documented that eighty-five percent of the parents fully supported the change and only ten percent wanted to return to letter grades.

Though public relations is a never-ending process, we were able to focus attention on other major areas of concern after that first year. As an administrator, you should keep abreast of the concerns within the community in order that you might address yourself to those concerns. Periodic parental surveys served well in our system.

FIGURE 6-5: Letter Grades

MEMO

TO: PARENTS
FROM: THE PRINCIPAL
RE: POSITION ON LETTER GRADES

Over the past year each of you has been invited to attend parent seminars at school, at which time we have discussed the validity of letter grades for reporting pupil progress. The purpose of this memorandum is to further clarify why we are moving to eliminate grades and to project alternatives which we feel will serve the needs of our students much better.

Generally, two major reasons for continued use of grades have evolved from our recent discussions:

1. Grades motivate students to work.
2. Grades report pupil progress to parents.

In the opinion of the West Elementary staff, neither of these reasons is valid, for there are better ways to provide this kind of information and to motivate students to work.

The idea that grades motivate students to work is perhaps the major reason why they should be eliminated. Using grades as motivation probably causes more harm than good. Grades are extrinsic in nature and too often become an end in themselves. Teachers and parents urge students to work for good grades, thus grades become the important objective and learning is reduced to a secondary status.

Every child is born with a natural instinct for learning, commonly known as curiosity. Failure to cultivate this natural instinct causes, or in some instances forces, educators to resort to external devices to motivate students to work and grades probably head the list. Once this external motivation is removed from the arsenal of educators, it will cause them to seek other means for motivating students to work. It will cause them to once again appeal to the instinctive desire and learning will take on new meaning. If one would but consider the amount of learning that takes place from birth to age six, when there are no grades, report cards, etc., one would realize that grades are not needed to motivate students.

If you have attended a parent seminar, you have already identified some of the fallacies of the grade system as a means of reporting pupil progress. In a more traditional approach where predetermined standards were set for each grade level, it might have been possible to report the degree of attainment of those pre-determined goals. However, as we move into programs which are geared to the needs of the individual, standards must be set which are commensurate with the ability and background of each individual, and grades can no longer serve that purpose.

It has been clearly demonstrated that different teachers read their own values, background, and prejudices into grades without ever realizing it, thereby confusing the issues completely.

For these reasons the West Elementary School Staff will replace grades with parent-teacher conferences and/or narrative reports. Through such conferences or narrative reports, teachers will be able to point out your child's strengths and weaknesses and make suggestions on what can be done toward improvement.

FIGURE 6-6: Report Card

WEST ELEMENTARY SCHOOL

PROGRESS REPORT

DR. A. W. DENNIS
Superintendent

RAYMOND CLARKE
Principal

PARENTS: Enclosed you will find a report of your child's progress. If there are any questions please contact the school and a conference will be scheduled.

MATHEMATICS

The table below will help you to determine the progress your child is making in math. The solid blocks indicates that there are no study-guides at that level while the numbers indicates how many study guides there are to be completed. You can determine exactly what each study guide includes by referring to your Pre-High School Information Guide. The teacher has placed an "X" in the space that your child has completed this reporting period.

AREA OF CONCERN	A	B	C	D	E	F	G
Numeration	8	7	3	2	4	2	6
Place Value			2	3	3	3	3
Addition	3	10	5	8	3	1	3
Subtraction	1	2	3	5	1	1	1
Multiplication			1	6	7	7	3
Division			1	5	5	3	2
COP			4	5	5	4	3

AREA OF CONCERN	A	B	C	D	E	F	G
Fractions	1	3	3	3	4	4	4
Decimal Fractions						3	5
Money			3	4	5	4	
Time			3	3	5	1	1
Measurement			3	2	1	4	3
Geometry			3	1	1	5	6
Special Topics			1	3	2	5	

The following check list will provide you with additional information on your child's strengths as well as areas where he she may need to improve. A rating scale will be used from 1-5 with one being no and 5 meaning yes.

No				Yes	
1	2	3	4	5	Assumes responsibility
1	2	3	4	5	Should be working at home in his/her study guides
1	2	3	4	5	Needs to drill on basic addition facts at home
1	2	3	4	5	Needs to drill on basic subtraction facts at home
1	2	3	4	5	Needs to drill on basic multiplication facts at home
1	2	3	4	5	Needs to drill on basic division facts at home

Your child has worked _____ # of _____ study guides or packets since the last reporting period.

NARRATIVE REPORT

Name of student _____ has completed his _____ year in school and will re-enter next fall as a _____ year student.

FIGURE 6-6: Report Card (cont.)

Student _____ Teacher _____ Date _____

Unit _____ Year In School _____

LANGUAGE ARTS LOWER ELEMENTARY

This area of the curriculum includes reading, spelling, writing, listening skills, speaking skills as well as other communications skills.

NARRATIVE REPORT

ITA

The teacher will check the blank as the child completes a given section.

Phase I	Phase II	Phase III
1. Rides	6. Book 4	8. Book 6
2. Dinosaur Ben	7. Book 5	9. Book 7
3. Houses		10. Workbook 8
4. Book 2		
5. Book 3		

Follow Up Program In ITA

11. Words and Their Structure _____
12. Thinking ....
13. Writing ....
14. Punctuation ....
15. Reference ....
16. Lab Manuals: This section is optional with each teacher. If it is used the teacher should circle the correct manual completed.

    1 2 3 4 5
    6 7 8 9 10

BASIC SOCIAL PROGRAM

This area of concern includes both social studies as well as the social development of your child

SOCIAL STUDIES NARRATIVE REPORT

The check list below will help to further pinpoint your child's areas of strengths as well as the areas that need improvement. A rating scale of 1-5 will be used with 1 meaning no and 5 meaning yes with 2, 3 & 4 meaning some degree in between. This applies to social studies and science.

No   Yes

1 2 3 4 5	Turns in assignments on time
1 2 3 4 5	Learning to use reference materials
1 2 3 4 5	Learning concepts that he will be able to apply in life
1 2 3 4 5	Completes outside assignments
1 2 3 4 5	Is developing a sense of responsibility and/or self-direction
1 2 3 4 5	Is able to apply the scientific method in daily living.

Social Development

1 2 3 4 5	Works well with other students
1 2 3 4 5	Is developing a good concept of him/herself
1 2 3 4 5	Is developing good citizenship traits
1 2 3 4 5	Is learning to listen to and follow directions
1 2 3 4 5	Is not learning well because of a disciplinary problem
1 2 3 4 5	Talks too much
1 2 3 4 5	Is cooperative and participates well in music
1 2 3 4 5	Is cooperative and participates well in PE

SCIENCE NARRATIVE REPORT

Alternate Methods of Reporting as a Means of Motivating Students

The best public relations effort that any school could develop would be to have children who are happy and enjoy school. Since the major thrust of this entire concept is to improve learning through improving the child's self-concept and promoting self-direction, there is no problem in accomplishing this objective. With the elimination of grades, tests are no longer used to grade children. Much of the pressure and related problems brought on by use of grades, which teachers and students experience, will disappear. The students will be happier as a result of the more relaxed atmosphere as intrinsic motivation gradually replaces the extrinsic devices.

Teachers will begin to view tests as diagnostic instruments rather than as devices to grade children, thus the programs will take on a diagnostic-prescriptive approach. Students will be placed in the curriculum at a level commensurate with ability and achievement. Promotion and failure will become a thing of the past, for children will work on a given skill or concept until it is mastered then move on to the next. Continuous progress will indeed become a reality as the child begins each year exactly where he left off the previous year. If a child is sick for a month or two, he will not get hopelessly behind. Students will become involved in their own learning from which positive attitudes will evolve. Parents will begin to notice the changing attitudes of their children toward school and this will help to solidify parental support.

Summary

At a time when instruction is changing from a group-oriented approach to an individually-oriented approach, attention is being focused upon procedures for evaluating and reporting pupil progress since letter grades will no longer serve that purpose. Alternatives must be found and while this is being done there will be a certain amount of concern on the part of teachers and parents. The implications for administrators are quite clear. You must take steps to modify the attitudes of parents and teachers who may hold to tradition.

A good public relations program will provide the vehicle for modifying attitudes of parents. You, as the administrator, will be aware of the time and energy that will be required. Though there are no absolute answers that will work in every situation, a few suggestions have been provided in this chapter that will be helpful.

1. Identify the specific things you wish to accomplish and establish the underlying reasons.

2. Be prepared to offer appropriate alternatives.

3. Initiate an aggressive public relations program which will involve parents, not merely inform them.

4. Keep in touch with your parents and be aware of their concerns. This can be accomplished effectively through the use of parental surveys.

IMPROVING STUDENT INVOLVEMENT
WITH TEAM PLANNING

Students must become actively involved in the learning process before any learning is realized. The primary function of the teacher is to find a way to actively involve students in the learning process. This can be accomplished through many avenues. Just as there are many roads to Rome, there are many paths to learning. However, some may be more interesting, involving, and lasting than others. It is this involvement which encourages the mind to inquire, to seek and strive to know, which creates an intrinsic urge to delve more deeply, to ask why and why not.

Stimulation with a team approach can be a more exciting and varied way to instill a personal and singular involvement with each child. The personalization of an individualized approach allowed by team teaching creates an atmosphere for enhancing a child's self-concept. Once the student realizes that he is important and is endowed with personal worth, then academic progress can be improved as the student becomes involved in the learning process.

Student Involvement—The Key to Success

One of the most crucial problems facing educators is that of motivating students. Every teacher has at some time taught students who were quite successful just as they have attempted to teach those who were less successful. The key factor that made the difference was the motivation of the student. It would appear that many of today's students are turned off in the classroom, while educators, seeking solutions, often become frustrated when they fail to reach the students. As a change agent, you should remember that the major problem lies in adequately identifying the problem. If you fail to pinpoint the problem, the solutions which are applied will probably not have the desired results, and in fact, may further complicate the problem.

Today's youth are living in a permissive, affluent, and enlightened society. What motivated students in the past may hold little appeal today. Too often we tend to rely upon refined versions of extrinsic motivation. It should be acknowledged that there is a place for limited use of extrinsic motivation in the field of education, but the very foundation of our educational programs should not be premised on extrinsic motivation, lest it become an end in itself rather than a means to an end. Behavior modification is a classic example of an extrinsic device which appeared to be an answer, but it has not yet achieved the desired results because the concept was misunderstood and/or inappropriately applied. To find the solution, teachers and parents must recognize that just as teachers cannot "learn a child anything," neither can they educate him. Every student must assume the responsibility for his own education, but too often we operate on the premise that this is the responsibility of the teacher or the school. It will be necessary for these roles to be reversed, and for the responsibility for education to be placed upon the individual. This will be the first step toward bringing about the kind of student involvement which will be needed.

Students must learn to accept responsibility for their actions. This can be learned only through allowing students to assume responsibility, make decisions, and learn to live with those decisions. Teachers should help students recognize the consequences of unwise decisions and help them to determine how alternatives may have affected the consequences in a particular situation.

For example, in the math program at our school the students were free to work through the study guides either individually or with a friend. They had access to the keys for checking their work at will. Initially, this caused some concern among a few of the teachers because it provided the students an opportunity to cheat. The teachers were encouraged not to become overly concerned but to use this as an occasion to help the students see that they were cheating no one but themselves. When the students realized that they could not pass the post-test because they had not satisfactorily completed the work required, they understood, perhaps for the first time, that making unwise choices was always accompanied by consequences which usually meant a double effort on their part. This was much more effective than having the teacher tell a student it is wrong to cheat. Thus, making decisions and accepting the results contributes to the maturation process and the building of personal integrity within each student.

This concept should be interwoven throughout the curriculum with appropriate checks and balances. It calls for a shifting of responsibility with evaluation of classroom techniques. Such an evaluation will be achieved through the team approach involving teachers, parents, administrators, and students.

One of the reasons why students neglect to assume the responsibility for their own learning is that too often we stress the cognitive skills at the expense of the affective skills. It is

recognized that individuals in our society have need of certain cognitive skills, but it should be remembered that there
are affective skills which children begin to develop early in
life which need further development before or in conjunction
with the cognitive skills. As a change agent, you must find a
way to place these two important concepts into their proper
perspective, for to do otherwise would result in a substandard
educational program.

In our school we took definite steps to insure that the affective skills were developed along with the cognitive skills.
We identified two very basic objectives in the affective domain and made certain that adequate attention was given to
these objectives as noted below:

1. To promote a better self-concept
2. To promote more self-direction

These two broad objectives are vital and must be given
proper attention before a student can learn the cognitive
skills effectively. Once a child "feels good about himself,"
and will assume the initiative, academic progress can be
made.

Curriculum materials were developed in such a manner
that students would be expected to assume more responsibility for their own learning, therefore we were able to
develop self-direction as we taught the cognitive skills.
Details of such curriculums will be spelled out in Chapters
Eight and Nine. As self-direction was stressed it also helped
to improve the self-concept of students who previously had a
poor self-concept. If these two vital affective areas can be improved, then a gradual increase in academic achievement can
be documented.

Team Planning Can Improve
Student Participation

If students are to become involved, they must accept the
responsibility for their own learning. Once they begin to assume responsibility for their own learning, they will have

taken the first step toward bringing about the kind of involvement which will be needed to promote more self-direction, which is the key to self-motivation.

As a change agent, it is vital that you fully comprehend the implications and the changes that will take place in the schools across the nation once students begin to assume the responsibility for their own learning. Motivation would cease to be a problem, for students would become self-motivated. Report cards, grades, grade levels, as well as many other extrinsic devices, would disappear from the educational scene as students begin to learn for the purpose of satisfying their curiosity. We see this kind of learning every day outside the confines of the school.

How can this responsibility be shifted from the teacher to the student? There are several things that can be done through a team approach. Through team planning teachers will have an opportunity to project ideas which will be carefully analyzed by fellow team members and the better ideas will prevail while others will be eliminated. This critical analysis of teachers' ideas by fellow teachers may cause some concern in the beginning, but this concern will gradually give way to a more professional attitude. This kind of team interaction will result in an improved instructional program for students.

Programs must be developed which will place the responsibility on the individual. This can be done by providing alternatives in the *process* of learning a given skill rather than in *which* skill will be learned. Checks and balances such as the one in the previous statement will keep a student's options within an acceptable limit and insure that all of the necessary skills are learned. Such programs must be developed in such a way that individual students can move ahead as rapidly as they are able, or move as slowly as is necessary to insure mastery of skills. This will mean that students in a given class may be working on many different things at the same time which necessitates a well-developed management and control system. In addition, diagnostic procedures will need to be incorporated into the program to insure that each student spends his time on skills which he needs. An in-depth description of programs of this nature will be given in the next two chapters.

Improving the Student's Self-Concept Through Involvement

It is important that students believe in themselves. If a student lacks confidence in his ability, he is seriously handicapped. Not every student in a given class will lack this self-confidence, but those who do, need help. There are several things that can be done for temporary relief, but steps should be taken to insure permanent relief over a long period of time.

Developing individualized programs where students are placed at a level at which they can succeed is the best assurance that the student's self-concept will be enhanced. There is much truth in the adage that "success breeds success and failure breeds failure." Students must be placed in situations where they can be successful. This means that predetermined standards will no longer serve any useful purpose, for standards must be commensurate with the individual. In the absence of predetermined standards, letter grades cannot be used to report pupil progress; therefore, alternative methods of evaluating and reporting pupil progress will need to be found. This was dealt with in depth in Chapter Six. Once the student realizes that he can be successful, he will move ahead to accomplish other tasks that he once thought impossible.

When these ideas were applied in our school, we successfully reversed a negative trend in academic achievement. Through reorganizing curriculum we stressed self-direction, and this brought about student involvement which resulted in an improved self-concept and improved academic achievement. This is noted in Figure 7-1, an excerpt taken from the validation report conducted by the Alabama State Department of Education and Auburn University.

FIGURE 7-1: ValidationReport

" . . . the earlier a child enters the program [the Math Program described in Chapter Eight] or the longer he participates, the more successful he will be. An examination of the data reveals this point clearly . . . "

" . . . in a regular program it would be much more likely that these children would, at the end of three years in school, be another two or three years behind. Rather, 65.9 percent of them, as a result of participation in the program, experienced 2.5+ years of growth . . . "

" . . . The validation team concludes that the mathematics component of the Title III Program was successful beyond the objectives set for that program. Furthermore, the validation team proposes that the program was much more successful than the evaluation data suggests . . . "

Promoting Self-Direction
While Improving Student Progress

One of the major concerns of the critics of American education has been that when students finish school they are often unable to assume the responsibilities of adulthood and make mature, intelligent decisions. Our educational system has traditionally been so oriented toward the "right answer syndrome" that we have unconsciously taught students to rely upon others to make decisions. Suddenly, after twelve years of school, we expect them to assume responsibility and make intelligent decisions without having given them the proper skills.

We must organize educational programs so that students will be placed in decision-making roles and will be expected to assume responsibility throughout their educational career. Generally, our present system operates on the premise that if we educate our citizenry, they will be in a position to make intelligent decisions. Actually, we should operate on the premise that education results from decision-making. This would give a slightly different slant and bring about basic changes in our educational system.

Curriculum can be organized in such a way that students will be expected to assume more responsibility and make decisions concerning their education which will result in a more self-directed individual. This system will allow the student the opportunity to assume responsibility while learning the cognitive skills.

Instructional situations need to be developed which will place students in problem-solving roles where they will be expected to consider alternatives. Such situations can be created and implemented very well in a team approach, and students will not only learn the basic cognitive skills, but they will also become more self-directed and better able to assume their rightful place in society.

Summary

The key to success for any student is involvement. To bring about the kind of involvement required to "turn students on" will necessitate the re-ordering of priorities in eduction. First, it will be necessary that each individual student assume the responsibility for his education rather than the school assuming it for him. Secondly, educators must eliminate superficial goals for students and appeal to that intrinsic desire burning within each individual. To accomplish this goal, educators must make some very basic changes. Such changes will not require large expenditures of money, but will require alterations in attitude. Once this is accomplished, students will learn to live and function in a democratic society and the superficiality of our present educational system will be stripped away and we can, in fact, "get back to the basics."

FACULTY TEAM PROCEDURES FOR INDIVIDUALIZING MATHEMATICS

The key to developing a realistic, non-graded program which will promote self-direction and allow students to proceed at a rate commensurate with their ability and past performance lies in the organization and development of curriculum. Adequate attention must be given to this vital area of concern in order that management systems can be developed which will allow teachers and students to follow a sequential program in any discipline area.

Basic Components
for Individualizing Mathematics

Mathematics is one area of the curriculum which will lend itself to a completely individualized approach, provided the following key components are incorporated into the design:

1. Continuum of Skills to be Learned

2. Diagnostic Instruments to Determine Specific Skill Needs for Each Individual
   a. Pre-test
   b. Individual Skill Test
   c. Post-test

3. Developmental Activities
   a. Study Guides
   b. Supplementary Activities

4. Tracking techniques to Monitor Pupil Progress
   a. Student's Daily Math Record Card
   b. Class Profile Card

5. Implementation Procedures to Insure Continuity

6. Accountability Control Techniques

Each of these six components will be discussed in depth in the remainder of this chapter and the functions of each component will be described.

The diagram in Figure 8-1 will illustrate the learning cycle utilized in this math program.

FIGURE 8-1: Learning Cycle

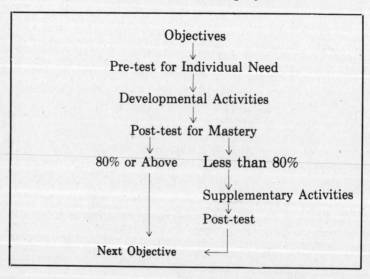

Mathematics Continuum
for Curriculum Organization

The first step toward the development of an operational non-graded math program is to determine exactly what is to be learned. This can be accomplished in the area of math through the development of a continuum of skills. Such a continuum will not only give scope and sequence, but it

FIGURE 8-2: Organizational Chart

Area of Concern	A	B	C	D	E	F	G	H
Numeration	8	7	3	2	4	2	6	
Place Value	0	2	3	3	3	3	0	
Addition	3	10	5	8	3	1	3	
Subtraction	1	2	3	5	1	1	1	
Multiplication	0	0	1	6	7	7	3	
Division	0	0	1	5	5	3	2	
Combination of Processes	0	0	4	5	5	4	3	
Fractions	1	3	3	4	4	4	0	
Decimal Fractions	0	0	0	0	3	5	0	
Money	0	3	4	5	4	0	0	
Time	0	2	3	5	1	1	0	
Measurement	0	1	2	4	3	2	0	
Geometry	1	3	1	1	5	6	0	
Special Topics	0	0	1	3	2	5	0	
Total number of skills	14	35	36	56	50	41	18	250

should also provide the necessary structure which will eliminate the possibility of gaps. The continuum of skills described herein was organized under fourteen major areas of concern as illustrated in Figure 8-2. Each block as noted under the various levels in Figure 8-2 will show the exact number of skills identified at that level. The skills are organized in a sequential spiraling manner with each subsequent level advanced in difficulty over the preceding level.

CONTINUUM OF SKILLS

The partial list of skills which follows will illustrate the manner in which the skills were organized. This is a necessary component of any manageable, individualized instructional program. The complete list of skills in Levels A—G can be found in the appendix.

Numeration Level A

1. After completing this study guide, the student will be able to count to ten by ones.
2. After completing this study guide, the student will be able to read numbers up to ten.

Numeration Level B

1. After completing this study guide, the student will be able to read and match numerals one through ten.
2. After completing this study guide, the student will be able to read numerals from 0 to 100 and will be able to count from 1 to 999 by ones.

Numeration Level C

1. After completing this study guide, the student will be able to read and write numerals 1-200. He should be able to fill in sequence of numbers from any starting point.
2. After completing this study guide, the student will be able to supply a number one more, less, or between 1—200.

Numeration Level D

1. After completing this study guide, the student will be able to read and write numerals to 1,000 starting from any point.
2. After completing this study guide, the student will be able to skip count by 3's, 4's, 5's, 10's, 100's, and 1,000's (or any other number) beginning from any point.

Development and Organization of Diagnostic Tests and Testing Centers

Once all the skills to be learned have been identified and properly sequenced, it will be necessary to develop diagnostic procedures to determine the specific needs of each student. These diagnostic procedures were interwoven throughout the program by use of three types of assessment instruments.

1. Pre-test or pre-assessment

2. Individual skill tests

3. Post-tests or post-assessment

All of these assessment instruments were located in the diagnostic testing center and administered to students as needed.

DIAGNOSTIC TESTING CENTER

During the initial stages of implementation, all tests were administered by the classroom teachers in their respective team areas. This created a monumental task for the classroom teachers for they were expected to administer, score and record all test data, and to work with each individual student within the team area. It soon became evident that a different approach would be necessary if the program was to be a manageable one.

This is a classic instance where several teachers were ready to declare the program a failure and return to the

traditional approach. As a change agent, you should be
careful that management problems are not used as excuses
for discontinuing an otherwise sound idea. When it became

FIGURE 8-3: Math Pre-test

MATH PROGRAM

Level __D__   Pre-test Name_____
Skill _Numeration_   Date_____

1. Directions: Write the missing numerals,
   counting by ones.

A. 964, 965, _____, 967, _____, _____, _____, 971
b. 501, 502, _____, _____, _____, _____
c. 347, 348, _____, _____, _____
d. 94, 95, _____, _____, _____, _____
e. 798, _____, _____, _____, _____, _____

2. Directions: Write the missing numerals,
   counting by threes or fours
   depending upon the proper sequence
   shown below.

A. 3, 6, _____, _____, 15, _____, _____
B. 8, 12, _____, _____, 24, _____, _____
C. 69, 72, _____, _____, _____, 84, _____
D. 228, 232, _____, _____, _____, _____, 252
E. 203, _____, 209, 212, _____
F. 130, _____, 138, 142, _____

evident that the program was unmanageable,we started looking for alternatives. Out of this search evolved the idea of a
centralized diagnostic testing center staffed with paraprofessionals. All diagnostic tests were located in one side of one of
the learning centers, which served as a diagnostic testing
center during the math classes. All tests were administered,
scored, and returned to the classroom teacher. The teacher
analyzed the results and made the appropriate diagnosis,
then instructed the student as to what was needed next. This
diagnostic testing center relieved the teachers of a tremendous task. From that point, support for the program increased among staff members.

PRE-TEST

The pre-test was designed to assess the skill needs of
each student. For example, a pre-test was developed to
diagnose which of the eight skills in Numeration Level A the
student needed. Each of the eight skills was scored as an individual test and the scores recorded on the Student's Daily
Math Record Card under the column entitled Pre-test
Results, as illustrated in Figure 8-8. This enabled the teacher
to see at a glance the exact skill which was needed. Figure 8-3
is a representative sample of a pre-test which was used for
Numeration Level D. Since there were only two skills at that
level, the pre-test is divided into two parts and each scored
individually.

INDIVIDUAL SKILL TEST

The Individual Skill Tests were designed to help the
teacher and the student determine whether or not a given
skill had been mastered after the student completed the
study guide for that particular skill. After a student completed a study guide he or she was sent to the diagnostic
testing center with a note instructing the aides which test
should be administered. The aides administered the appropriate test, scored it, and returned it to the teacher. The
teacher analyzed the test and recorded the results on the Student's Daily Math Record card (Figure 8-8) under the
heading entitled Individual Skill Test Results. If the student

made 80% or more on the test, he or she moved on to the next
skill as illustrated in Figure 8-1. The teachers were free to exercise their professional judgment regardless of the grade, but
they were expected to note any deviation from the guidelines
agreed upon earlier. The scored tests were filed in the student's folder for future reference and for auditing purposes.

The Individual Skill Test prevented students from working too long without getting some indication of their progress
and it enabled the teachers to monitor the student's progress
as they moved through the program. A sample of the Individual Skill Test has been illustrated in Figure 8-4.

FIGURE 8-4: Individual Skill Test

MATH PROGRAM

Individual Skill Test

Level   D   Name_____
Skill   Num.1   Date_____

Directions: Fill in the blanks below by completing
the sequence.

A. 50, ____, 52, ____, 54, ____, ____, ____
B. 98, ____, 100, ____, ____, ____, ____
C. 174, 175, ____, ____, ____, ____, ____
D. 895, 896, ____, ____, ____, ____, ____
E. 990, 991, ____, ____, ____, ____, ____

Allow four points for each correct blank.

POST-TEST

After the completion of all skills in a given area of concern, the teacher and the student mutually decided whether or not the student was ready for the post-test for that area of concern. If so, he or she proceeded to the diagnostic testing center for the final check for that area of concern. The post-test closely paralleled the pre-test but was slightly altered for obvious reasons. This final check for mastery was administered by the aides, graded, and returned to the teacher. After analyzing the post-test, the teacher recorded the results under the column entitled Post-Test Results on the Student's Daily Math Record Card. If, in the opinion of the teacher, the student had successfully mastered all skills in that area of concern, it was so noted on the record card and the student proceeded with the pre-test in the next area of concern and the cycle was again repeated as illustrated in Figure 8-1. If, on the other hand, the student did not perform as well as the teacher deemed necessary for mastery, the teacher was expected to determine the cause and take steps to remedy the problem. The teacher often referred the student to supplementary activities in the study guide or in some other source which would enable the student to learn the skill. In some instances the teacher may determine that the student needs more time and/or maturity before the skill can be mastered. If this is the case, the teacher so notes the student's record and allows him or her to move ahead. Figure 8-5 illustrates a sample post-test.

FIGURE 8-5: Math Post-test

Math Program

Level ___D___   · Name_____
Skill _Numeration_ Post-test Date_____

---

1. Directions: Write the missing numerals,
             counting by ones.

A. 95, 96, ____, ____, ____, ____, ____
B. 984, ____, 986, ____, ____, ____, ____
C. 344, 345, ____, ____, ____, ____, ____
D. 898, ____, ____, ____, ____, 903, ____
E. ____, 103, 104, ____, ____, ____, ____

---

2. Directions: Write the missing numerals,
             counting by threes, or fours,
             depending upon the sequence.

A. 8, 12, ____, ____24, ____, ____, ____
B. 3, 6, ____, ____, ____, ____, ____
C. 69, 72, ____, ____, ____, ____, ____
D. 4, 8, 12, ____, ____, ____, ____, ____
E. 2, 5, ____, ____, ____, ____, ____

Format for Organizing Curriculum Materials

In order to manage an individualized instructional
program the curriculum materials had to be organized into

some format that would enhance availability and/or accessibility of such materials for teachers and students. This task was accomplished by organizing curriculum materials into study guides, one for each skill identified in the continuum. This organization provided materials for teaching the skills identified through the diagnostic test. Once the skill need was determined, the materials were available through the study guide to help the student learn that skill. Several options were usually written into the study guides from which the students could make certain choices. This placed the students in a decision-making position. As they learned their cognitive skills, self-direction was promoted.

The study guide has been identified as a set of self-directed materials designed to assist the student in learning a given skill or concept through the use of a variety of media. There were three essential parts of the study guides as developed by the West Elementary Staff—the cover page, the activity page, and the work pages. Each of these parts will be expanded upon in depth.

COVER PAGE

For the beginners it was felt that a cover page would be helpful. The cover page was designed for Levels A and B to attract the attention of the students in the first and second year levels. The study guides were written in such a way that little reading was required at the first year level. While they functioned well in the program, the teachers read the instructions to a child until he learned to read. Also peer tutoring, in which the teachers called upon fourth and fifth year students to work with the beginners was used. While many of our visitors were concerned about the beginning reader, we found no problem in their functioning in the program.

For levels C through G the cover page was not used because of the added expense involved in printing.

ACTIVITY PAGE

The activity page for each study guide included the objective for that particular study guide as well as the developmental activities. The objective was printed at the top of the page along with the identifying data. The developmental activities were listed directly below the objective. (See Figure 8-6.) These activities were designed to teach the skill and make it possible for the student to assume the initiative once the skill need had been determined. Many of the students were able to take the study guide and follow the instructions entirely on their own while others needed more teacher direction. This arrangement provided for more self-direction since the student did not have to wait for the teacher unless he needed help.

A variety of activities was written into the study guides to provide the students with certain options such as selected references to a textbook, filmstrips, filmloops, tapes, and special seminars which were conducted by the principal, the music teacher, and the P.E. teacher. All of these people were certified in elementary education and were, therefore, fully qualified to conduct the seminars.

The classroom teachers periodically identified areas in math which they felt needed additional attention. The seminars were designed around the areas of greatest need as identified by the classroom teacher. Any student needing those skills was free to attend the seminar. While this could be interpreted as a form of achievement grouping, it was, in our opinion, providing an opportunity for any child to get additional concentrated help if he needed it, and no student was in the seminar for more than one or two weeks at a time.

It should also be noted that volunteer parents were used to conduct seminars in the areas of addition, subtraction, multiplication, and division facts which require a great deal of drill.

The activity page used in the study guides is illustrated in Figure 8-6.

FIGURE 8-6: Sample Activity Page

Math Program

Level ___D___   Name_____

Skill   Num. 1   Date Begun_____

Individual Skill Test Results____   Parent's Sig._____

Objective

After completing this study guide, you should be able to read and write numerals to 1,000 starting from any point.

Developmental Activities

1. Study the objective carefully and be certain that you understand its meaning. See your teacher if you do not understand it.
2. Choose one of the following text book selections and work it. Attach the work to this study guide.
   a. Laidlaw, Patterns In Mathematics, Book 3 (Red) page 63
   b. Houghton Mifflin, Modern School Mathematics, Book 3 (Red) Pages 11, 14, & 18
3. You will need an abacus or place value chart from the learning center for some of the activities in this study guide. Complete the work pages in this study guide.
4. If you need more help on this study guide you may wish to preview filmstrip # 37. You will find it in the learning center.
5. See filmloop F.L. 19 Place Value in the library.
6. Check your work by the key located in your classroom.
7. See your teacher about the Individual Skill Test for this study guide.

WORK PAGES

In addition to the developmental activities listed on the activity page, several work pages were included in each study guide. Figure 8-7 will illustrate a typical work page.

FIGURE 8-7: Math Work Page

Math Program	
Level _D_	Name _____
Skill _Num. 1_	Date _____
Work Page	

Directions: Fill in the missing numerals.

1. 453, 454, 455, ___	2. 353, 354, 355, ___
3. 821, 822, ___, 824	4. 721, 722, ___, 724
5. 613, ___, 615, 616	6. 402, ___, ___, ___
7. 125, ___, ___, ___	8. ___, ___, 398, 399
9. ___, 900, ___	10. ___, 700, ___, ___
11. 652, ___, ___,	12. ___, 756, ___, ___
13. 723, ___, ___	14. 1, 2, ___, ___, ___,
15. 99, ___, ___	

Management Systems
for Monitoring Pupil Progress

The success of any individualized instructional program will depend upon an effective management system. The Student's Daily Math Record card noted in Figure 8-8 served an important function in the management system. It enabled the classroom teacher to monitor each child's progress without the use of complex systems which most school systems may not be able to obtain. This same card has been effectively used with other commercial programs which are currently on the market.

This record card was kept on each student. The diagnostic test scores were recorded in the appropriate space. This enabled the teacher and student to determine at a glance exactly what was to be worked by each student. It also provided the teacher with valuable information which proved helpful during parent-teacher conferences, for skill deficiencies could be pinpointed easily and suggestions made for improvement.This card was filed at the end of each school year and the student resumed exactly where he left off the previous year.

The class profile card pictured in Figure 8-9 was kept by each teacher on the students in a given class. It was used in the audit process to help the program auditor determine at a glance the students whose records need close examination to determine if they were working to capacity. It also enabled the teacher to keep a summary of progress on her entire class.

As principal, I occasionally audited teachers' math records. Through the use of the class profile card I was able to spot the children who were having difficulty. After reviewing their individual record, I was in a position to take appropriate action to correct the problem if one existed.

Recommended Implementation Procedures

The implementation procedures described below were designed for a semi-open school with cross-grade grouping. However, the program has been implemented successfully in a traditional graded school with slight variations of the implementation guides.

To insure continuity in implementation of the program, the guidelines were drawn up by the principal and submitted to the Instructional Policy Committee for approval. After the

FIGURE 8-8: Student Profile Card*

FIGURE 8-9: Class Profile Card*

CLASS PROFILE

MATH

Student's Name	L E V E L	N U M .	PV LA AL CU EE	A D D	S U B .	M U L .	D I V .	F R A C .	D E C .	F R A C .	M O N E Y	T I M E	M E A S .	G E O .

Note: When a child completes a given area of concern, indicate the proper
level by shading or coloring. This profile will cover four different
levels.

Instructional Policy Committee approved the guidelines, every teacher was expected to follow them explicitly. To prevent excessive structure, all teachers were free to deviate as they determined the need, but they were expected to justify the change with a brief note on the student's record card. The following implementation guidelines, taken from the Teachers' Handbook, will give you some idea how the program was operated in our school.

MATH IMPLEMENTATION GUIDELINES

In order for this Individually Guided Math Program* to be successful, it will be necessary to implement it uniformly throughout the school. To assure uniformity in implementation, the following procedural steps have been approved by the Instructional Policy Committee.

INITIAL PROCEDURES

** The first two weeks of school will be devoted to review and the initial pre-testing.

** All students previously in the program should be pre-tested in the same level in which they were working at the end of the previous year and in the area of concern immediately following the one completed the previous year.

** All new students entering our school for the first time should be pre-tested in numeration. It will be left to the teacher's discretion as to which level new students should begin.

** Initially, the pre-test may be administered individually or collectively depending upon the needs of the class.

** Following the initial pre-testing during the first two weeks, all other diagnostic testing will be handled in the diagnostic testing center.

** Each teacher must carefully analyze each child's test paper after it is scored to make certain the kinds of errors the child is making.

** Each student will need a new Student's Daily Math Record Card each year. The previous year's card will be filed for reference.

** Every teacher's records will be audited by local program auditors at the end of the initial testing to make certain that every teacher is ready to begin the program.

* Copyright 1970 University of Wisconsin
  Permission for use granted by
  National Computer Systems, Inc.

CLASS ORGANIZATION

The testing center will be operated for the Upper Elementary and the Lower Elementary math programs. Each teacher will be assigned approximately twenty-five to thirty students by the team leader. This teacher will serve as math advisor to her homeroom group, see that they progress reasonably well through the program, provide guidance as needed, and evaluate and report student progress to parents as required by the reporting procedures.

SEMINARS

Seminars will be conducted on a regular basis for the Upper Elementary division. These seminars will be conducted by the principal, the music teacher, the P.E. teacher, and in some instances by aides and/or volunteer parents. These seminars will be centered around difficult areas of concern which generally cause students excessive problems, such as long division. The topics will be determined by the classroom teachers based upon their greatest need. Once the topics have been determined all teachers will be notified and will be permitted to send any student who, in their opinion, needs to attend. The students will remain in the seminar as long as they feel a need at which time they will return to their team area and continue to work on an individual basis.

ACCEPTABLE LEVELS OF MASTERY

The acceptable level of mastery will ultimately be left to the teacher's discretion, for in the final analysis only the teacher can determine when a given student has satisfactorily mastered a given skill. However, it is strongly urged that at least 80% mastery be expected. In some areas of concern a higher level may be expected while in other areas a lower level of mastery might be acceptable. If teachers accept anything less than 80%, however, they should justify it with a brief note stating their reasoning.

FIGURE 8-10: Math Audit Form*

Note: Please indicate the type audit performed by
checking the appropriate space below.
____ Complete Audit (Carefully check every child's
record)
____ Spot Audit (Check every third or fourth record)
____ Specific Purpose Audit (State the Purpose)
. . . .
Teacher _____ Unit _____
Date Audited_____ Audited by_____

Yes No N/A

____ ____ ____ 1. Have all diagnostic tests been administered as designated in the
guidelines?
____ ____ ____ 2. Have the pre-test scores been
recorded correctly?
____ ____ ____ 3. Have the individual skill test scores
been recorded correctly?
____ ____ ____ 4. Are all Individual Skill Test scores
80% and above or accompanied with
an explanation?
____ ____ ____ 5. Have the post test scores been given
before the student moves to the next
area of concern?
____ ____ ____ 6. Are all post-test scores 80% and
above or accompanied with an explanation?
____ ____ ____ 7. Have the appropriate study guides
been assigned as determined by the
pre-test?
____ ____ ____ 8. In your opinion, is this teacher attempting to follow the guidelines?

Accountability Techniques to
Insure Proper Implementation

The accountability techniques were designed and approved by the Instructional Policy Committee to insure proper implementation and control. This procedure also provided teachers with information and suggestions for improving their classes. Every teacher's records were audited periodically by the team leader, the principal, or some other designated individual. The audit form as noted in Figure 8-10 will indicate the kinds of things that were checked during an audit. An audit report was given to each teacher following the audit with suggestions on what might help to improve the situation.

Summary

The individually guided math program described in this chapter has been nationally recognized and disseminated throughout the nation. It was successfully implemented in graded schools with self-contained classrooms as well as in non-graded, open-space schools. The prototype design upon which the program was developed offers extensive flexibility, for it can be altered slightly for use in any setting from the traditional to the most recent innovative schools. It is a diagnostic-prescriptive program in nature with a management system that can be used very effectively by any classroom teacher. The management system has been utilized with other commercial programs currently on the market.

There are six essential components incorporated into this design:

1. Continuum of Skills (See Appendix)
2. Diagnostic Procedures
3. Developmental Activities
4. Monitoring System
5. Implementation Procedures
6. Accountability Control Procedures

These are key factors which should be incorporated into any design which purports to meet the specific needs of individual students. Since the program is based entirely upon the specific needs of the individual, the grouping technique utilized is of little concern.

This design allowed for uniform implementation within the school system. The auditing techniques employed assured a certain amount of control over the implementation within each teacher's classroom. In addition, the program provided teachers with a very systematic approach to the teaching of mathematics while allowing for optimum flexibility.

FACULTY TEAM PROCEDURES FOR INDIVIDUALIZING LANGUAGE ARTS

The Language Arts Program is one of the most comprehensive and challenging curriculum areas in which you, as a change agent, must provide leadership in developing a well-structured, sequential program. This part of the curriculum includes the essential communication skills which all students must develop to function effectively in society.

Identification of Basic Areas of Concern in the Language Arts Program

To provide the necessary structure to this important area of curriculum, the West Elementary School Staff subdivided the communication skills in to seven essential areas of concern as follows:

1. Listening Skills
2. Speaking Skills
3. Grammar Skills
   a. Punctuation Skills
   b. Alphabetizing Skills
   c. Capitalization Skills
   d. Organizing Skills
   e. Dictionary Skills
   f. Parts-of-Speech Skills
4. Writing Skills
   a. Creative Writing
   b. Handwriting Skills
5. Reading Skills
   a. Word Attack Skills
   b. Comprehension Skills
   c. Study Skills
6. Library Skills
7. Spelling Skills

This diverse phase of the curriculum requires a multi-approach because of the nature of each of the areas of concern. Each area must be considered in its own unique way. For example, an area such as creative writing will not lend itself to a diagnostic-prescriptive approach as well as the grammar skills; therefore, each of the basic areas which has been identified will be treated as an entity in itself in the remainder of this chapter.

Listening Skills

Although specific skills were identified for the area of listening, no formal attempt to diagnose specific skill needs in this area of concern has yet been developed. Teachers were provided with a complete listing of the listening skills and used a "check-off" system to indicate mastery as the informal evaluations were made by the teachers. The partial listing of the listening skills below will illustrate the format on which these skills were organized.

Listening Skills (Partial Listing)

After completing the assigned activities, the student will show that he/she can:

Level A

1. follow oral directions for drawing pictures.
2. follow directions in dictating a sentence to the teacher describing a picture, an object, or an experience.
3. follow directions in making a copy of your name.

Level B

1. follow directions in arranging pictures and objects in a predetermined order.
2. follow directions for playing games.
3. follow directions in marking worksheets.

Speaking Skills

This phase of the communications skills was organized and implemented in a very similar manner to the listening skills. No formal effort has been made to develop a diagnostic-prescriptive approach for this area, although the skills were identified and made available to the teachers. Teachers utilized the resource materials available and informally evaluated and recorded the student's performance.

Grammar Skills

The mechanics of grammar overlap all the various phases of the communications skills and cannot be taught entirely in isolation. However, the grammar skills have been identified and properly sequenced. These skills were subdivided into six groups:

1. Punctuation Skills
2. Alphabetizing Skills
3. Capitalization Skills

4. Organizing Skills
5. Dictionary Skills
6. Parts-of-Speech Skills

Under the six subheadings the specific skills were identified and appropriately sequenced at the various levels. Since this phase of the communications skills will lend itself well to a diagnostic-prescriptive approach, the West Elementary Staff developed a systematic approach to insure that all the grammar skills were taught. This approach included five major components and made it possible to completely individualize the grammar skills. These components were:

1. Continuum of Skills
2. Diagnostic Techniques—Pre-test
3. Developmental Activities
   A. Study Guides
   B. Supplementary Activities
4. Evaluation Procedures—Post-test
5. Management System—Student's Record Card

These five components were used in the development of a manageable program to insure that all the grammar skills were given adequate attention. Each of the components will be described in depth and their function outlined in the next few pages.

CONTINUUM OF SKILLS

The first and perhaps most challenging step is to determine exactly what is to be learned and organize it in some manner which will give not only scope and sequence, but will provide structure for a systematic approach which must be developed to insure a continuous and uniform implementation of this phase of the curriculum. The sample skills printed below will give you some indication regarding the organizational format used. While it is recognized that there are many ways in which the skills could be organized, it is necessary that some structure be developed to provide a systematic approach. The partial list of grammar skills below will be printed in full in the appendix.

Grammar Skills

Level C

PUNCTUATION

After completing this study guide, you should be able to:

1. use a period after abbreviations and initials.
2. write sentences using a question mark correctly.
3. use correct punctuation in writing a date.

ALPHABETIZING

After completing this study guide, you should be able to:

1. arrange words into alphabetical order according to the first letter of the word.
2. locate names and numbers in a telephone directory.

CAPITALIZATION

After completing this study guide, you should be able to:

1. write sentences, beginning each with a capital letter.
2. capitalize initials and titles (including Mr., Mrs., and Miss).

ORGANIZING SKILLS

After completing this study guide, you should be able to:

1. use the correct heading on your daily work.
2. use the correct form in writing a letter.

DICTIONARY SKILLS

No skills identified yet.

DIAGNOSTIC TECHNIQUES

The second most important step in the development of an individualized approach is the development of diagnostic procedures to determine the specific skill needs of each individual. Once the continuum of skills has been completed a diagnostic test must be developed for each skill identified. This is a time consuming process but not particularly difficult. When developing such diagnostic tests you should keep one thing uppermost in mind—the objective for which you are developing the test. When such tests are completed, the teacher is in the position to diagnose the skill need. The student is expected to make at least 80% or above on the pre-test or work through the study guide. Figure 9-1 exemplifies a typical pre-test used in our program.

FIGURE 9-1: Pre-Test

LANGUAGE ARTS

Level C <u>Punctuation</u>   Name _____
Skill <u>#1</u>   Date _____

Pre-test

Directions: Write the contraction for these words. The sample word is written correctly.

Sample: is not isn't

1. was not _____
2. did not _____
3. could not _____
4. does not _____
5. you are _____
6. has not _____
7. have not _____
8. can not _____
9. would not _____
10. I am _____

Each correct answer is worth 10 points.

DEVELOPMENTAL ACTIVITIES

The organization of the developmental activities is an important managerial factor which must be reckoned with if the classroom teacher is going to be able to implement the program effectively. Once students are free to move at their own pace and work on levels commensurate with their ability, they will spread out on the continuum of skills. This could mean that a given teacher will have thirty students working on thirty different skills. Unless curriculum materials have been properly arranged, the teacher will find it very difficult, if not impossible, to manage the program. For this reason we chose to organize our developmental activities into study guides—one for each skill identified. Once the skill need of a given student was diagnosed, the curriculum materials were readily available for the students. The students were able to select the appropriate study guide and begin working on that particular skill. If the student needed the help of the teacher, it was available but if he could proceed on his own, he was free to do so. This provided the teacher with more free time to concentrate on students who were having difficulty.

Each of the study guides included two essential components, the activity page and four to eight work pages. The activity page included the objective along with a list of developmental activities designed to help the student learn the skill as illustrated in Figure 9-2.

FIGURE 9-2: Activity Page

LANGUAGE ARTS

Level C <u>Punctuation</u> Name_____
Skill   <u>#5</u>   Date _____

Activity Page

Objective

After completing this study guide, the student will
be able to use the apostrophe in contractions.

Developmental Activities

1. In *English Is Our Language* (3) Read and
   study the exercises on pages 179-181.

2. *My Study Book For English Is Our
   Language:* Work pages 81 and 82.

3. Complete the pages in this study guide and get
   your teacher to spot check your work.

4. If you feel that you need extra work complete the
   following:
English (3) Pages 208—215
English is Our Language (3) Pages 122, 133, 191
English For Meaning (3) Pages 176, 177, 199, 200

5. You should now be ready for your post-test.

Note: For other materials refer to Wisconsin Word
      Attack Skill B 10.

The work pages included with the study guides provided
curriculum materials through which the students were expected to work as illustrated in Figure 9-3.

FIGURE 9-3: Work Page

LANGUAGE ARTS

Level C <u>Punctuation</u>   Name_____
Skill   <u>#5</u>   Date_____

Work Page

Directions: Work the following activities. Read
           each one carefully

Key: Many contractions are made with the word
     "not"

   example: do not   don't

   When you make contractions the "o" in not is
   dropped and an apostrophe is added as in the
   example above.

   Complete the following:

1. does not   doesn't

What letter is left out? ____ What was used to indicate that it was left out? ____

2. did not   didn't

What letter is left out? ____ What was used to indicate that it was left out? ____

Write, in your own words, a rule which will help you
to remember how to write contractions using not.

_____

_____

_____

EVALUATION PROCEDURES

After the student completed a study guide, the post-test was administered to determine the level of mastery. Eighty percent or above was required, but teachers were free to expect more, or accept less, if they determined it to be necessary. If, however, the student did not make eighty percent or above, supplementary work was assigned. The supplementary work included alternate activities which were included on the activity page or some other activity that the teacher wished to assign.

No sample of the post-test will be illustrated, but it is very similar to the pre-test. It is altered slightly for obvious reasons.

MANAGEMENT SYSTEM

To effectively implement programs of this nature, it will be necessary to develop some techniques for tracking pupil progress. This should be done in conjunction with the reorganization of the curriculum. The procedure developed for this phase of the Language Arts was a modified version of the math profile card as described in Chapter VIII. The six areas—punctuation skills, alphabetizing skills, capitalization skills, organizing skills, dictionary skills, and the parts of speech were substituted for the areas of concern as illustrated in Figure 9-4.

FIGURE 9-4: Profile Card

Name of Student _____ Date _____ Teacher _____

Grammar Skills

LANGUAGE ARTS PROFILE CARD

AREA OF CONCERN	LEVEL	PRE-TEST RESULTS	POST-TEST RESULTS
Organizing Skills			
Dictionary Skills			
Parts of Speech Skills			
Punctuation Skills			
Capitalization Skills			
Alphabetizing Skills			

Writing Skills

The ability to communicate through the medium of writing has in effect enabled past generations to transcend death and live into the future. The development of this medium of communication has been the most important development in the history of mankind and it will continue to play a vital role for many generations to come. Therefore, any institution charged with the responsibility of developing such skills for the youth of today would be derelict in its duty if it failed to give adequate attention to such an important area of concern.

The West Elementary School Staff divided this area into two subdivisions—creative writing and handwriting. Creative writing is the most important of the two subdivisions for it deals with a student's ability to express his thoughts in a readable form. To provide systematic procedures toward the development of these skills, the staff identified and sequenced the objectives. However, due to the abstractness of creativity no attempt was made to develop a diagnostic approach to this phase.

Copies of the continuum were made available to teachers along with appropriate study guides for each skill identified. The students worked through all of the study guides. The evaluations were subjective in nature and the teachers simply indicated on a "check-off card" that the students had worked through the respective skills. The study guides were organized on the same format as those for grammar skills and math skills.

Handwriting, initially, was left to the discretion of the classroom teacher. No formal effort was made to identify formal skills, or the diagnostic approach, as in the area of grammar skills, but commercial handwriting books were available to each of the respective teams if they desired them.

However, in the long-range planning, some effort will be focused upon developing a more systematic approach to this area of curriculum.

Reading Skills

The reading program is another diverse area of the Language Arts Program which will require a varied approach to develop this broad range of skills. The following programs and/or materials were used in our school:

Initial Teaching Alphabet i/t/a
Economy Materials
Wisconsin Reading Design
Talking Page
S R A Reading Materials
Listen and Think Tapes
Barnell Loft Materials
Supplementary Textbooks
Sullivan Programmed Readers
Reading Machines

On the next few pages two of the major phases of the reading program will be discussed in depth—the i/t/a and the Wisconsin Reading Design.

The Initial Teaching Alphabet was used in the Lower Elementary Division. This medium was developed by Sir James Pittman in England and was designed to be used in the initial stages of a student's reading career. The approach consists of three basic phases through which the student must work. The first phase introduces the student to the i/t/a characters. The second phases teaches the student to read using the i/t/a characters while the third and final phase leads the student through a gradual transition.

Instead of the traditional twenty-six letters in the alphabet, there are 44 symbols or characters which represent the 44 basic sounds. After the student learns the 44 characters and the sound each represents, he is able to "sound out" almost any word that he can say. This enables the child to use a larger vocabulary both in his reading and in his creative writing. It builds confidence in the vital stage of the student's development because he experiences success early and does not get hopelessly lost in trying to learn all of the various combinations of letters which make up all of the basic sounds. The student can begin to read and experience success early while the maturation process will allow him to better handle the traditional orthography as he begins to make the transition. Research indicates that the i/t/a students generally spell better than non-i/t/a students.

The time required for the transition will vary depending upon the individual. Most students make the transition during the first year; others will complete it during the second year, while a few will continue into the third year. The teachers on our staff report that the i/t/a may not be the best approach with students who have auditory perception problems. However, it is doubtful that any phonetic approach would serve best where there are auditory perception problems.

Figure 9-5 will illustrate the record keeping system that the teachers use for each of their i/t/a students. This record is passed on to teachers as the student progresses through the primary grades. It is also reproduced on the student's narrative report in order that the student's parents will know how well their child is progressing.

FIGURE 9-5: ITA Chart

ITA READING PROGRAM				
Phase One: Teaches the students the ITA characters.				
Rides		Book 2		
Dinosaur Ben		Book 3		
Houses				
Phase Two: Teaches the students to read in ITA.				
Book 4		Book 5		
Phase Three: Student makes the transition from ITA to regular alphabet.				
Book 6		Book 7		
Workbook 8				

The Wisconsin Reading Design is a prototype design which provides the structure for teaching some of the basic reading skills. It is used in grades one through six in our system. There are three basic phases of this design—the word attack skills, the study skills, and the comprehension skills. While it is not recognized as a complete reading program, it does provide a systematic approach to learning the basic skills.

There are four essential components, each of which will be discussed and illustrated in the next few paragraphs. They are:

1. Continuum of Skills
2. Diagnostic Procedures
   a. Pre-test
   b. Individual Skill Test
3. Teacher Resource Kit—Developmental Activities
4. Management Procedures—Student Profile Card

CONTINUUM OF SKILLS

Specific skills were developed for each of the three areas identified—the word attack skills, the study skills, and the comprehension skills. After the skills were identified, behavioral objectives were written for each of them. Beginning on page 143 you will find a complete listing of all the skills, although space will not permit a complete listing of the behavioral objectives at this point.

DIAGNOSTIC PROCEDURES FOR WISCONSIN SKILLS

To determine specific skill needs of each student the pre-test was administered. The pre-test covered all of the skills at a given level. This enabled the teacher and student to know exactly which skill was needed. After working through the activities or study guide designed to teach a given skill, the individual skill test was administered to determine mastery. If the student had mastered the skill, his card was notched by the appropriate skill as illustrated in Figure 9-6. If the student failed to master the skill, his card was not notched. This allowed the student a second chance at learning the skill at some future time.

TEACHER RESOURCE KIT—
DEVELOPMENTAL ACTIVITIES

Another one of the major components of the Wisconsin
Reading Design was the Teacher's Resource File. A resource
folder was developed for each of the skills identified. It included a list of published materials which would help in the
development of that particular skill, work pages which could
be reproduced, as well as other suggested activities for
teachers to utilize if they needed them.

It should be noted that this program was not developed
by our school. We became involved with this program
through Dr. Foster Watkins from Auburn University who was
working at that time as a consultant from the Southeastern
Educational Laboratory, Atlanta, Georgia. Our school was
selected as a pilot school in the early stages of development of
the Wisconsin Program. Members of our staff did help to key
the curriculum materials that were available in our school to
the various skills identified.

Following the initial stages of the pilot project, we
developed study guides for each of the skills. The study
guides were developed on the same format as the grammar
skills and math skills. This reorganization of the
developmental activities gave us more flexibility in the implementation process.

MANAGEMENT PROCEDURES—
STUDENT PROFILE CARD

All the skills were printed on a card as illustrated in
Figure 9-6. The results of the pre-test were recorded in the
center of the card and each of the skills mastered as indicated
by the pre-test was notched.

All the profile cards of the students in a given team were
grouped together. A skewer was passed through the hole
beside Skill #1. All students who had passed that skill on the
pre-test and had their card notched were sifted out of the
stack of cards. This left only those needing that particular
skill. These students were grouped with one or two teachers,

depending upon the number involved. They stayed with that teacher from one to three weeks where they concentrated their attention on that one skill only. After the students mastered that skill, their card was notched and they were never pulled for that skill again. This is a classic example of students being grouped according to skill need. The groups were flexible and continuously changing. It sometimes became necessary for a student to repeat a given skill if he failed to master it the first time around.

FIGURE 9-6: Word Attack Profile

Student Profile Card—Developed by the University of Wisconsin

WISCONSIN DESIGN FOR READING SKILL DEVELOPMENT

© 1972-The Board of Regents of the University of Wisconsin System   V36037X

LEVEL A:
- 1 Rhyming words
- 2 Rhyming phrases
- 3 Shapes
- 4 Letters, numbers
- 5 i — Colors
- 6 Words, phrases
- 7 Initial consonants
- All A skills

WORD ATTACK

NOTE: Skills marked i are assessed by a performance test or teacher observation.

LEVEL C:
- 1 i — Sight vocabulary
- 2 Consonant variants
- 3 Consonant blends
- 4 Long vowels
- 5 Vowel + r , a + l , a + w
- 6 Diphthongs
- 7 Long & short oo
- 8 Middle vowel
- 9 Two vowels separated
- 10 Two vowels together
- 11 Final vowel
- 12 Consonant digraphs
- 13 Base words
- 14 Plurals
- 15 Homonyms
- 16 Synonyms, antonyms
- 17 i — Independent application
- 18 Multiple meanings
  All C skills

WISCONSIN DESIGN FOR READING SKILL DEVELOPMENT

PUPIL NAME   DATE

UNIT	GRADE	SPECIAL CODE	LEVEL

SKILL	RS	M	% C

LEVEL B:
- 1 i — Sight vocabulary
- 2 i — Left-right sequence
- 3 Beginning consonants
- 4 Ending consonants
- 5 Consonant blends
- 6 Rhyming elements
- 7 Short vowels
- 8 Consonant digraphs
- 9 Compound words
- 10 Contractions
- 11 Base words
- 12 Plurals
- 13 Possessives
  All B skills

DATE	NO. OF SKILLS	GROWTH

LEVEL D:
- 1 i — Sight vocabulary
- 2 Consonant blends
- 3 Silent letters
- 4 Syllabication
- 5 Accent
- 6 Unaccented schwa
- 7 Possessives
  All D skills

A similar method was used to monitor student progress with study skills and comprehension skills.

All the other programs and/or materials mentioned in this chapter will not be discussed in depth, but they were used to provide a complete reading program.

Library Skills

All the library skills were taught by the librarian during specially scheduled library periods. The librarian worked closely with all the different teams to provide a systematic presentation of the library skills beginning as early as the first grade. The details will be presented in Chapter XII.

Spelling Skills

At this time no formal effort has been made to develop a spelling continuum per se, but the teachers within a given team planned and executed their own spelling program by using available textbooks.

Summary

The diversity of the Language Arts Curriculum necessitates a wide range of approaches. Since this important area deals with the communications skills, it is one of the most important areas with which any staff must deal. The greatest challenge lies in developing the format in which the skills must be organized. There is no one way to organize the skills, but until some kind of organization is decided upon, there can be no systematic approach to teaching those skills. For this reason the West Elementary staff arbitrarily decided to organize the skills under the following major areas of concern:

1. Listening Skills   4. Writing Skills
2. Speaking Skills   5. Reading Skills
3. Grammar Skills   6. Library Skills
          7. Spelling Skills

Additional subdivisions were organized under these major headings. While the West Elementary staff has not yet developed a diagnostic prescriptive approach to all areas of concern, progress has begun in the area of grammar and reading. Our efforts will continue as time permits.

WORD ATTACK SKILLS *

LEVEL A

1. Rhyming words
2. Rhyming phrases
3. Shapes
4. Letters, numbers
5. Words, phrases
6. i—Colors
7. Initial Consonants

LEVEL B

1. i—Sight vocabulary
2. i—Left-right sequence
3. Beginning consonants
4. Ending consonants
5. Consonant blends
6. Rhyming elements
7. Short vowels
8. Consonant digraphs
9. Compound words
10. Contractions
11. Base words
12. Plurals
13. Possessives

LEVEL C

1. i—sight vocabulary
2. Consonant variants
3. Consonant blends
4. Long vowels
5. Vowels +r, a + l, a + w
6. Diphthongs
7. Long and short oo
8. Middle vowel
9. Two vowels separated
10. Two vowels together
11. Final vowel
12. Consonant digraphs
13. Base Words
14. Plurals
15. Homonyms
16. Synonyms, antonyms
17. i—Independent application
18. Multiple meanings

LEVEL D

1. i—Sight vocabulary
2. Consonant blends
3. Silent letters
4. Syllabication
5. Accent
6. Unaccented schwa
7. Possessives

STUDY SKILLS

LEVEL A

1. PT—Representation
2. Positions of objects
3. Measurement: size

LEVEL B

1. Picture symbols
2. Picture grids
3. Measurement: distance
4. Graphs: relative amounts

LEVEL C

1. Nonpictorial symbols
2. Color keys
3. Number—letter grids
4. Measurement: size
5. Measurement: distance
6. Graphs: exact amounts
7. Graphs: differences
8. Tables: relative amounts
9. Tables: one cell
10. PT—Book skills
11. Alphabetizing

LEVEL D

1. Point and line symbols
2. PT—Cardinal directions
3. Scale: whole units
4. Graphs: difference
5. Graphs: approximate amounts
6. Tables: difference
7. Indexes
8. PT—Dictionaries and glossaries
9. Tables of contents
10. Alphabetizing
11. Guide words
12. Headings and sub headings
13. Selecting sources
14. Facts or opinions

LEVEL E

1. Point, line and area symbols
2. Intermediate directions
3. Scale: Multiple whole units
4. Graphs: differences
5. Graphs: purpose and summary
6. Tables: multiple differences
7. Tables: purpose and summary
8. Indexes
9. Dictionary meanings
10. Cross references
11. PT—varied sources
12. Guide words
13. Guide cards
14. PT—Notetaking
15. Specialized references
16. PT—books: special feature
17. Fact checking

LEVEL F

1. Maps: analysis
2. Map projections
3. Inset maps
4. Different scales
5. Graphs: differences
6. Schedules: relationships
7. Subject index
8. Dictionary pronunciation
9. Card filing rules
10. Dewey Decimal System
11. Outlining
12. Catalog cards

LEVEL G

1. Maps: synthesis
2. Latitude and longitude
3. Meridians and parallels
4. Scale: fractional units
5. Graphs: multiple differences
6. Graphs: projecting and relating
7. Schedules: problem-solving
8. Reader's Guide
9. Card Catalogs
10. Outlining

COMPREHENSION SKILLS

LEVEL A

1. *Identifies a topic: pictures*
2. *Determines sequence: first or last event*
3. *Uses logical reasoning*

LEVEL B

1. *Identifies a topic: paragraphs*
2. *Determines sequence: event before or after*
3. *Uses logical reasoning: predicts outcomes*
4. *Reads for detail*

LEVEL C

1. *Identifies a topic: paragraphs*
2. *Determines sequence: event before or after*
3. *Uses logical reasoning: determines cause-effect relationships*
4. *Reads for detail*

LEVEL D

1. *Identifies a topic sentence*
2. *Determines sequence: explicit relationship*
3. *Reasons deductively*
4. *Reads for detail*
5. *Uses context clues: unknown words*

LEVEL E

1. *Identifies a main idea: paragraphs*
2. *Determines sequence: implicit relationships*
3. *Reasons deductively*
4. *Reads for detail: sentences with one centrally-embedded part*
5. *Uses context clues: unknown words*
6. *Determines the meaning of prefixes*

LEVEL F

1. *Identifies a main idea: two paragraphs*
2. *Orders events along a timeline*
3. *Reasons deductively: indeterminate conclusions*
4. *Reads for detail: sentences with one centrally-embedded part and an introductory or terminal clause.*
5. *Determines the meaning of suffixes*

FLEXIBILITY OF SCHOOL PLANT TO ACCENTUATE TEAM PROGRAMS

In the first chapter, a plan of action for bringing about systematic change was outlined to serve as a guide to our total effort. Five major areas of concern were identified, one of which included renovation of the school plant. While the school plant design is not vital to the success of an individualized instructional program, it can enhance the entire operation by providing more flexibility.

Since West Elementary School was built in the early fifties in the traditional design, it was decided that minor renovations would create a more versatile learning environment. This chapter deals with the school design as it relates to the instructional process and offers suggestions concerning minor, inexpensive renovations which will provide the desired flexibility.

Advantages of the Open-Space School Design

The nature of individualized instruction necessitates a variety of activities taking place simultaneously among the students in a given classroom or team area. These diverse activities demand a more flexible plan for use of personnel, time, space, and materials. For example, a given team of teachers can organize, implement, and monitor many different activities with fewer materials more easily in an open-space facility than in the conventional classroom. This kind of learning environment enhances the opportunity for students to develop more self-direction and creates an atmosphere which is less distracting to students when visitors observe or pass through a team area. Such a physical setting provides for more efficient use of staff and materials through the team approach, which will ultimately result in more learning on the part of the student.

A word of caution—improper planning can render such renovations useless and, in fact, could create problems, unless adequate attention is given to the other major areas of concern such as attitude on the part of all people involved, including students, teachers, administrators, and parents; curriculum development; organization of instructional teams, and techniques for evaluating and reporting pupil progress. It should be remembered that open space is not vital to implementing a sound individualized instructional approach, but it can enhance such an approach if it is properly organized and understood.

Renovations of Conventional Plants
To Create Open Space

Renovations necessary to create the open space need not be elaborate or expensive. Most schools usually have non-supporting walls which can be removed completely or supporting walls through which a passage between the classrooms can be opened. Such simple alterations will provide the desirable flexibility which will enable both students and teachers to move freely between the areas. More elaborate renovations can be made if budgets will allow, such as carpeting and air-conditioning which will improve the learning environment and reduce the noise level.

Figure 10-1 illustrates a few simple renovation ideas for developing team areas or learning centers from the traditional design. Three alternatives are illustrated here but there are other possibilities.

FIGURE 10-1: Renovation Designs

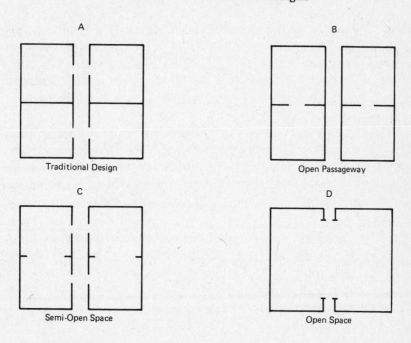

Figure 10-1A represents the conventional structure and severely limits movement within the area unless students and teachers move through the corridors, while figure 10-1B offers access between two rooms which provides a little more flexibility. Renovations of this nature are very inexpensive but will serve the purpose for anyone operating on a limited budget. Figure 10-1C will provide semi-open space facilities similar to those being used at West Elementary School, while figure 10-1D will provide the open-space facility which will accommodate a team of approximately 100 students and four teachers. This plan will increase the size of the team area by allowing teachers and students to utilize the corridor which is usually wasted space. With this plan it would be helpful to have outside doors in each team area.

Plans of this nature or some combination thereof can provide the open space needed at a relatively low cost to the school system.

West Elementary School, the school in which these programs were developed and implemented originally, was designed with a combination of the ideas illustrated in figure 10-1. The renovations were completed during the summer months when school was not in session, therefore there was no interruption of classes. The total expense involved in renovating West Elementary School, as noted in figure 10-3, did not exceed $3,000.00, excluding the carpeting and air-conditioning. For us such alterations were accomplished with a minimum use of capital outlay and no loss of class time.

Figure 10-2 illustrates the design of the floor plan prior to the renovations. There was no open space or semi-open space in the original design. Figure 10-3 will illustrate the floor plan after the renovations were completed.

FIGURE 10-2: West Elementary School
Prior To Renovation

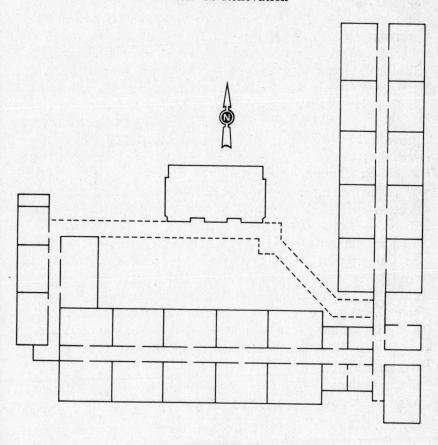

FIGURE 10-3: West Elementary School
After Renovations

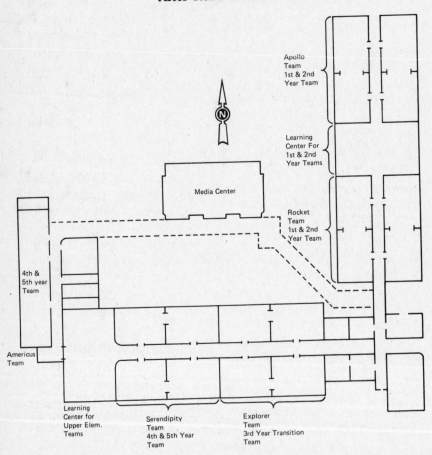

Attitudinal Problems
and How to Deal With Them

Parental and teacher attitude are crucial to the success of the open space concept. For this reason you, as a change agent, should be extremely concerned and take steps to insure a positive attitude from both groups.

A lack of understanding of the reasons for any change can create problems among staff members and the lay public. As a change agent, you will want to illustrate clearly the reasons why you wish to move to the open space concept. It should be noted that everyone wants to improve the learning opportunities for children, even those who oppose the innovative ideas. The apprehension among parents and teachers alike results from a lack of certainty of what the changes will bring. Therefore, be careful to challenge ideas rather than motives—often there is a very thin line between the two.

We focused attention upon attitude from the beginning, for there were a few teachers on the staff who were opposed to the open-space concept. Others were apprehensive but offered no strong resistance, but most of the teachers were willing to cooperate, while a few were pressing hard for the renovations. Those who were opposed to the proposed renovations attempted to use parental concern to halt the changes.

This opposition climaxed one evening when I received a phone call from the PTA president and was informed that a petition was being circulated to halt the planned renovations. I was informed that the major opposition was coming from one of my teachers. While I was privately outraged, I moved quickly to determine the depth of the opposition from parents and found that it was token, but I called for another parent seminar to be held at night to give everyone an opportunity to express themselves on the matter and to respond to any concerns which the parents may have held. All members of the Board of Education, the Superintendent of Education, the other principals in the system and the teachers on my staff were present except the one who had encouraged the parents to start the petition.

A few dissident parents expressed their concerns vigorously but the overwhelming majority helped to counter the opposition, for they had availed themselves of many of the seminars held earlier to involve parents. This early involvement proved to be worth all the effort we had put into it, for these parents came to our defense. Following that seminar all active opposition subsided and the proposed changes were approved and implemented.

Generally, parental attitude was very positive, for they were receptive to change once we had explained what we wanted to change and the reasons for the change. We found that parental attitudes were not nearly as polarized as that of the teachers. The attitude of dissenting teachers proved much more difficult to penetrate, but once the changes became a reality and the programs were implemented teacher support quickly solidified.

How an Individualized Program
Can Be Implemented
in a Conventional Setting

While the modern, open-space design will provide more flexible use of personnel, space, time and materials and create a more desirable learning atmosphere, it is not essential to the implementation of an individualized instructional program. In the event there are limitations on the budget which would prohibit renovations to provide open space, it should be remembered that the primary advantage of the team approach lies with the evolvement of the "true team spirit" which can be generated in any staff with the right kind of enthusiastic leadership. If adequate attention is given to attitude, curriculum development, and the other areas of concern mentioned earlier, the individualized approach can be implemented in the conventional classroom. When we, as educators, equate individualized instruction only with open-space facilities, we impose limitations upon ourselves. While the two concepts are not synonomous and the first does not require the second, they will complement each other.

The math program as described in Chapter Eight was implemented in the semi open-space facility, a completely open-space facility, and a more conventional facility all within the same system with a high degree of success. The one factor responsible for the success in all three settings was not the school plant design, rather it was the curriculum design and attitude of those responsible for its implementation.

The more conventional graded school in our system implemented the program by organizing a central diagnostic testing center in one of the extra classrooms, and used teacher aides to operate the center. The curriculum materials were made available to all teachers and students. The teachers within a given grade planned together as a team and implemented the program in their respective classrooms. The program worked well even though the teachers in the conventional school lacked some of the flexibility that the teachers enjoyed in the semi-open and the completely open-space facility.

Summary

The development and implementation of an individualized instructional program will necessitate several changes in the school setting. A few of these changes will be absolutely necessary, while a few will complement the endeavor but may not be essential. For example, attitude of staff, parents, administrators and students will be an essential factor with which you as a change agent must work. If the individual needs of students are to be considered, it will be necessary that a diagnostic-prescriptive approach be utilized in certain areas of the curriculum, therefore work on the curriculum design will be needed.

There are other factors which would enhance the entire operation but may not be critical. The school design is one example. The organization of teams and cross-grade grouping are examples of other changes which will enhance but are not critical factors.

ORGANIZING THE PROGRAM
AROUND THE MEDIA CENTER

In any well developed instructional program utilizing a team approach, the media center will become the hub around which much of the instruction will revolve. In such a setting the role of the media specialist is crucial. Primary involvements include assistance in curriculum development, curriculum implementation, and instruction in the proper use of library facilities and skills.

The Role of the Media Specialist
in Curriculum Development

Curriculum development is an important area in which media specialists should become involved, for they can offer valuable assistance to teachers, administrators, and supervisors as instructional materials are keyed to management systems.

As the teachers in West Elementary School began to

organize curriculum materials into a manageable format, the media specialist worked closely with them to make certain that teachers were aware of the materials available through the media center. The media specialist also served on the Quality Control Committee and the Instructional Policy Committee which placed her in the "center of the action". Placement on these key positions gave her a greater insight into classroom activities which enabled her to secure more appropriate materials.

A quality control questionnaire was developed for the teachers to provide guidelines for the development of the study guides. One of the key items on the questionnaire was as follows:

"In developing this study guide, did you consult with the media specialist to determine what materials were available through the media center?"

If the writer of a study guide was unable to answer in the affirmative, the study guide was returned along with instructions to see the media specialist. The media specialist also had further input as the study guides were evaluated by the entire Quality Control Committee.

The Role of the Media Specialist in the Implementation of the Discipline Areas

The role that the media center will play in the actual instructional process will be limited by the perceptiveness of the media specialist and/or the administrator in charge. The purpose of the media center as perceived by the media specialist will necessarily limit its usefullness in the instructional process.

In West Elementary School the media specialist played a vital role in the implementation process. After the study guides were developed, they were utilized by the teachers and students to guide the learning process. The study guide as defined in Chapter Eight was nothing more than management system to guide the student through a sequential and orderly process on an individual basis. If the study guide called for an activity such as a filmstrip, a tape, a filmloop or some other media, the student left his team area and went to the media center for that activity. The media specialist or an assistant worked with the student in locating and setting up the needed apparatus, thus the media specialist was involved in the day to day instructional process. It was not unusual for thirty to forty students to be in the media center during math working on some activity which was written into the study guides. This provided an opportunity for students to develop the needed library skills and helped to promote more self-direction.

The Instructional Role of the Media Specialist in Proper Use of Library Skills

Before students can develop the independence or self-direction desired it is necessary that they develop the necessary library skills. This endeavor becomes the joint responsibility of the classroom teacher and the media specialist. To provide continuity to such an endeavor the media specialists in our system developed a handbook outlining the skills and attitudes needed and the respective responsibilities of both teachers and media specialists for making certain that these skills were learned. The following list of library skills for lower elementary grades was taken from the handbook.

I. Citizenship

    A. Entering and leaving the media center quietly

    B. Browsing quietly

    C. Being polite

    D. Sharing materials

    E. Listening well during story hour

II. Building Lifetime Learning Skills

    A. Instill an enjoyment of good books

    B. Develop the ability and desire to pursue independent study

C. Create an awareness of sources of information other than books, such as magazines, filmstrips, recordings, and pictures

III. Care of Media

A. Turning the pages correctly
B. Handling all media with clean hands
C. Protecting media from damage by smaller children
D. Protecting media from weather
E. Learning to use proper bookmarks
F. Taking proper care of machines

IV. Use of Media

A. Learning correct procedure for checking books and other media in and out of the media center
B. Keeping books in correct order on the shelves
C. Learning how to identify fiction and non-fiction books
D. Introducing the location of fiction, non-fiction and reference books
E. Becoming aware of different classifications of books such as biographies, science, fairy tales, poetry, etc.
F. Using various devices (such as reading circles, reading ladders, etc) to encourage students to read a variety of subjects
G. Instructing teachers and students in the proper use of machines

V. Developing Study Skills

A. Discuss the parts of a book
B. Supplement the classroom teacher's instruction in the use of the dictionary and encyclopedia
C. Discuss how to write a short book report
D. Learn to give an interesting oral report
E. Become familiar with authors whose writings are suitable for lower grades
F. Introduce the card catalog
   1. How to use color-coded cards for all media
   2. How to locate media through the use of the card catalog by author, title, or subject
   3. How to find materials by their call numbers

Learning Center—An Extension
of the Media Services

When the instructional program is expanded to include greater utilization of materials through the media center as an integral part of the teaching-learning process it may be necessary to broaden that service. In West Elementary School two learning centers were created by removing two non-supporting walls as noted in figure 10-1D in the previous chapter. One of the learning centers as shown in Figure 10-3 served the two lower elementary teams and the second learning center served the upper elementary teams. The learning centers were multi-purpose rooms which housed the math diagnostic testing center, Title I classes, special education skill groups or any other activity requiring large open-space areas. Since it was difficult for all activities written into the study guides to be conducted in the confines of the team area and the media center, the two learning centers served as extensions to the media center. Many of the instructional materials and equipment which were too expensive to duplicate for each team area were located in the learning centers to which all teachers and students had access. When a student reached a point in a given study guide which called for an activity located in the learning center, he went to that particular area and completed that part of his assignment. This provided still another opportunity for students to develop more self-direction and to build mutual trust between student and teacher. It was very seldom that students abused the privilege.

When given the opportunity and trust, students will assume responsibility. The one factor that was noticed by visitors more than any other single factor was that the students, including first and second year students, were always busy and involved even though they were not under the direct supervision of the classroom teacher.

One note of caution to those who are operating on a limited budget—the key factor with which we are concerned is student involvement in the learning process. Student involvement can be obtained without a large expenditure of money. It should be remembered that when we at West Elementary School started to move toward the individualized concept we did not have any funding beyond a regular budget. As we moved further into the concept, additional funding was provided when we were able to show a need for it. It is possible for interest centers to be developed within a classroom. Such centers would provide students with the opportunity to become involved in activities which help develop initiative and promote self-direction. While more materials and open space will be helpful, do not close all possibilities because of budget problems. The programs being discussed in this book were developed to utilize materials which are usually available in every classroom, but they must be organized into some kind of management system similar to that which has been described in Chapters Eight and Nine.

The Instructional Policy Committee developed a general outline of the major areas of concern which were to be included in the social studies and science curriculum. (See example in Figure 11-1.) It should be noted that in the areas of social studies and science each team of teachers planned and implemented the various units of instruction within their respective teams. Each team planned the details of the units and determined their procedural process for implementing the different units. These activities varied at the discretion of the team members. They often included large group activities, small group activities, or individual projects.

The media specialist worked closely with the respective teams as they planned a unit of study. She helped to locate the available materials and checked them out to the various teams as they needed them. Other materials were placed on reserve for individual student or small group use within the confines of the learning centers or the media center.

Figure 11-1 will illustrate the outline for the science units through which the students were expected to work in their third, fourth, and fifth year in school. The social studies units were organized on a similar format.

FIGURE 11-1: Science Curriculum

MEMO

TO: TEACHERS
FROM: THE PRINCIPAL
RE: SCIENCE CURRICULUM

     The following outline of the various units in the area of science has been approved by the Instructional Policy Committee. The third, fourth, and fifth year students should work through each of these units during their last three years in this school.

I. Scientific Method—Orientation Unit (Levels C, D, & E)

II. Physical Science

    A. Simple Machines ....Level C & D
    B. Magnetism ....Level C & D
    C. Matter and Energy ....Level E & F

III. Biological Sciences

    A. Plants .... Level C, D, & E
    B. Animals .... Level C, D, & E
    C. Human Body
       1. The Body and Its Care .... Level C
       2. Health and Growth .... Level D
       3. The Body's Systems .... Level E

IV. Astronomical Sciences

    A. Solar System and Astronomy Level C & D
    B. Rocket and Space Travel ..... Level E & F
    C. Research and Discovery ... Level C, D, & E

V. Earth Sciences

    A. Earth and Water ....Level C
    B. Rocks and Their Formation .... Level D
    C. Oceanography and Weather ...... Level E

VI. Suggested Mini Units—suitable for any level:

    A. Manners   D. Safety
    B. Personal Hygiene   E. Seasonal Changes
    C. Food   F. Conservation
                    G. Pollution

FIGURE 11-2: Circulation Report

Give 1 to Principal
Give 1 to Mrs. Moore
Keep 1 for your files

ANNUAL LIBRARY REPORT
West Elementary School

	Books	Records	Filmstrips	Slides	Tapes	Transparencies	Vertical File Material	Pictures of Picture Units	Audio-Visual Machines
Circulation Record	44927	560	1587	121	4789	685	53 folders	556	193
Processing Record									

	8mm Filmloops	Globes	Maps	Needs and requests
Circulation Record				
Processing Record				

1. Books mended 472
2. Approximate number of pupils, outside of regularly scheduled classes, using library _____
3. Total classes in library 1,520
4. Number of classes taught by media specialist 836
5. Visitors this week _____
6. Additional comments:

Scheduling of Library Classes

The scheduling of library classes must be kept flexible in any school if the instructional process is to revolve around the media center. This kind of atmosphere can be severely limited by allowing rigidly scheduled classes to dominate the library program. The role of the media center is much broader than the traditional role of the conventional library which often became a place where children went once a week to check books in and out.

All regular scheduled classes were eliminated and children were encouraged to use the media center as a resource center as they needed it. In this manner the media center became an integral part of the instructional program. Arrangements were made to keep the media center open before and after school at which time students were permitted to borrow and return books or other media, do reference work or just browse.

Each of the team leaders worked with the media specialist to schedule classes for library skill instruction but no regular schedules were permitted. Figure 11-2 illustrates the circulation record for one year at our school. Such reports were submitted to the principal and to the superintendent each week. It will give some idea about the effectiveness of the library program in a school which worked its entire instructional process around its media center.

Summary

The concept of the traditional library has been expanded so that it includes the library as a resource center or media center around which the instructional program revolves. When this concept is put into practice, attention is focused upon the media specialist, whose role is expanded to include three important functions relating to instruction—curriculum development, curriculum implementation, and instruction related to proper use of library facilities including library skill development.

MAINSTREAMING OF SPECIAL EDUCATION STUDENTS

In recent years there has been a move to provide "special" education to meet the needs of exceptional students such as the gifted, the learning disabled, and the educable mentally retarded child. Many school systems across the nation have organized special schools or classes to meet the needs of these exceptional students. Though the intent was good, this procedure effectively removed many students from the mainstream of American education, and set up a caste system which has caused much concern among parents and educators. The current trend is to bring these students back into the mainstream.

The Case for Mainstreaming

In many educational circles the isolation of special students resulted from a genuine desire to make certain that our system of universal education applied equally to all students.

These efforts placed the exceptional children in a society of their own, while fellow students and many teachers looked upon them in a different manner from the "regular" student. It pinned undesirable labels on a large segment of exceptional children and unintentionally created a situation which, in effect, relegated the exceptional children to a secondary role in the classroom and perhaps in society. This deplorable situation served as the setting for many legal suits which evolved on both sides of the issue.

School administrators generally accepted the situation, for it usually provided additional funding, while the teachers accepted it because it removed atypical problems from the classroom. However, all knew in their hears that it was not the most desirable solution. After a few decades of this caste system, steps were taken to get these students back into the mainstream of American education. Efforts to reverse the trend proved to be frustrating to many administrators and teachers because legislation had been enacted which perpetuated the caste system, and attitudes had been formed which needed to be changed.

Alternatives to the 'Caste' System of Special Education

If the concept of individualized instruction is a valid one, then the need for isolating any child becomes a null issue except in the case of a few who would totally disrupt the teaching-learning process. As education officials begin to develop instructional programs which will meet the needs of individual students, the alternatives will become clear. When the instructional program is organized in a manner which is flexible enough to meet the needs of each child without having to isolate the exceptional student, academic and social needs can be met without causing unneccessary damage to the child.

Procedural Steps Toward Mainstreaming

As mentioned earlier, the attempt to move away from the practice of isolating "special" students can be frustrating in the absence of a definitive plan of action. There are two critical issues with which you as a change agent must work if you expect positive results—teacher attitude and curriculum design.

It is important that curriculum be re-organized in such a way that it will meet the individual needs of students. The math program and the language arts program as described in Chapters Eight and Nine exemplify such curriculum designs. Once this has been accomplished, teacher attitude becomes the next critical factor.

Placing special education students in a teacher's classroom does not mean that mainstreaming has been accomplished. Steps must be taken to change teacher attitude if there are any who reject the concept. At West Elementary School the practice of isolating the "special students" was challenged on the basis that it conflicted with our stated philosophy.

> "...we further believe that the school must provide instructional programs that will meet the needs of each individual..."

It was pointed out that an individualized program would meet the needs of all students, therefore the need to isolate any child based upon his special abilities or handicaps becomes a null issue, with the exception of those who would completely disrupt the teaching-learning process.

Following much discussion and debate on the issue, the memo shown in Figure 3-5 and re-stated in Figure 12-1, was issued to the staff as an important step toward mainstreaming.

The following year all special education students were assigned to regular homeroom groups. They were re-grouped with the special teacher for reading and math skill instruction. While this helped to remove much of the labeling, it did not remove all of it, since the students were being re-grouped with the special teacher for reading and math. A few of the regular teachers did not accept the idea completely for they felt that the special education teachers were not carrying their full load, but the practice continued for the sake of the students involved.

FIGURE 12-1: Mainstreaming

MEMO

TO: TEACHERS
FROM: THE PRINCIPAL
RE: MAINSTREAMING OF SPECIAL
              EDUCATION STUDENTS

In light of recent discussions it has become evident that we will not be able to reach a consensus of opinion regarding the mainstreaming of our special education students. Therefore, be informed that the following policy statement will become effective at the beginning of the next school year.

All special education students will be placed in the regular classroom. The special education teacher will serve in a tutorial capacity. All students identified as needing special help will be pulled from the regular classroom for math and reading, but will participate in all other activities in which other students participate. All students will be involved in P.E. classes, homeroom activities, lunch, music, and the basic social program.

Further details will be passed on to you as soon as they are available. I would appreciate your cooperation in this matter. In my opinion and in the opinion of the majority of this staff this policy will improve the learning environment for all concerned.

Almost without exception, the special education students started performing beyond previous levels and the attitude of the students was greatly enhanced. They were working in the same programs as the "regular" students but each at their respective level. Parental acceptance of the services of the special education teacher increased and there were no further problems getting parents to accept such services.

FIGURE 12-2: New Team Organization

```
┌──────────────────────────────────────────────────┐
│              Lower Elementary Teams               │
│          First and Second Year Students           │
│                                                    │
│  Rocket Team              Apollo Team              │
│                                                    │
│  1 Team Leader            1 Team Leader            │
│  3 Regular Teachers       3 Regular Teachers       │
│  1 Title I Teacher        1 Special Ed. Teacher    │
│                           1 Title I Teacher        │
│  100 Regular Students     85 Regular Students      │
│   0 Sp. Ed. Students      15 Sp. Ed. Students      │
├──────────────────────────────────────────────────┤
│              Third Year Transition Team            │
│                                                    │
│                  Explorer Team                     │
│                                                    │
│               1 Team Leader                        │
│               2 Regular Teachers                   │
│               1 Sp. Ed. Teacher                    │
│               1 Title I Teacher                    │
│                                                    │
│               80 Regular Students                  │
│               10 Special Ed. Students              │
├──────────────────────────────────────────────────┤
│              Upper Elementary Teams               │
│           Fourth and Fifth Year Students          │
│                                                    │
│  Serendipity Team         Americus Team            │
│                                                    │
│  1 Team Leader            1 Team Leader            │
│  3 Regular Teachers       2 Regular Teachers       │
│                           1 Sp. Ed. Teacher        │
│  100 Regular Students     85 Regular Students      │
│                           15 Sp. Ed. Students      │
└──────────────────────────────────────────────────┘
```

Incorporating Special Education Teachers
Into the Mainstream

The three special education teachers in our school worked together as a team in the basic skills area of reading and math. For example, all three of the special teachers worked with all the special students during math period. While this was an improvement over previous efforts, it did not eliminate the labeling. We moved to institute the second step of our plan by placing the special teacher in three of the five existing teams and assigned the special students to those three teams. By incorporating the special education team into the regular teams we were able to further eliminate the labeling of students. The schedule in Figure 12-2 illustrates the new team format.

Summary

Since universal education is the goal of this nation, any system of public education operating within it is honor bound to insure that every child receives that which he deserves. So that the many children with special abilities or liabilities are not neglected, legislation has been enacted which would insure that their needs are met. This worthy objective has resulted in the removal of a large number of atypical children from the mainstream of American education, thus denying them equal opportunity. This situation has given rise to a number of law suits. It has succeeded in isolating and labeling students, assuring many of them of secondary roles in the classroom and perhaps in our entire society.

Realizing the mistake, educators have begun to challenge this practice and move all children back into the educational mainstream. Since adverse attitudes have been formed, and legislation enacted, educators are faced with a frustrating problem as they move to correct the situation. As the trend continues, steps must be taken to get appropriate legislation, and as a change agent, you will need to work on two essential areas of concern—attitude and curriculum design.

APPENDICES

MATH CONTINUUM

LEVEL A

Numeration

After completing this study guide, you will be able to:
1. count to 10 by ones.
2. read numbers up to 10.
3. write number sequences through 10.
4. identify sets consisting of numerals 1-5 by writing or circling the numeral that names the set and by circling a set for a given number.
5. identify sets consisting of numerals 1-10 by writing or circling the numeral that names the set and by circling a set for a given number.
6. identify zero as the number of the set which has no objects by writing or circling the numeral that names the set and by drawing a set for a given number.
7. count orally using ordinal numerals, first through tenth, and circle an object corresponding to a given ordinal.
8. demonstrate adequate command of the concept of the following words: before, after, smaller, larger, equal; and the symbols $<$, $>$, and $=$.

Place Value

No objectives at Level A.

Addition

After completing this study guide, you will be able to:

1. recognize equivalent and non-equivalent sets and numeral words one through ten and be able to match objects in one-to-one relationships.
2. recognize the plus and equal sign, do addition through number 6, and find missing addends.
3. use the number line to add numbers.

Subtraction

After completing this study guide, you will be able to:
1. recognize the minus sign and do subtraction through number 6.

Multiplication

No objectives at Level A.

Division

No objectives at Level A.

Combination of Processes

No objectives at Level A.

Fractions

After completing this study guide, you will be able to:
1. recognize an object of a set divided into halves and to understand that 1/2 means one of two equal parts of an object or of a set. You should also know the meaning of the words "whole" and "one-half".

Decimal fractions

No objectives at Level A.

Measurement

No objectives at Level A.

Money

No objectives at Level A.

Time

No objectives at Level A.

Geometry

After completing this study guide, you will be able to: recognize a circle, square, rectangle, and triangle.

Special Topics

No objectives at Level A.

LEVEL B

Numeration

After completing this study guide, you will be able to:
1. read and match numerals 1-10.
2. read numbers from 0 to 100. You will also be able to count from 1 to 999 by ones.
3. write the numerals 1-100 in order. You will be able to count to 100 by tens.
4. identify cardinal numbers of any group to 100.
5. show relationship of tens and write their names.
6. use < (less than) and > (greater than) symbols in a group.
7. use ordinals through tenth.

Place Value

After completing this study guide, you will be able to:
1. write one and two place numbers shown by counting men and fill in blanks showing the value of one and two place numbers.
2. indicate that you know the meaning of the value of the numbers in three places by writing the numeral for the number shown by counting men and by filling blanks showing the value of each number.

Addition

After completing this study guide, you will be able to:
1. circle number picture addition from 0 to 10.

2. use $+$, $-$, and $=$ in number sentences to make them correct. You should be able to fill in the missing sums and addends.
3. use the number lines for adding numbers 0-10 and to find the missing addend.
4. find the sums and addends using numbers to 10. You should also learn how to add using 3 addends.
5. use $=$ or $\neq$
6. select other names for numerals.
7. better understand how addition and subtraction are related.
8. understand that the order of the addends in an equation does not change the sum.
9. solve one-step word problems.
10. use the following words: sum, addends, equals, does not equal.

Subtraction

After completing this study guide, you will be able to:
1. solve subtraction equations using numbers 0-10. You should understand that the sum is usually written first in a subtraction equation and that any time the sum is missing, you may add the addends to find the correct answer.
2. circle subtraction names for the number of objects in a set. You should be able to put $=$ or $\neq$ in subtraction equations to make them correct. You should be able to solve one-step word problems.

Multiplication

No objectives at Level B.

Division

No objectives at Level B.

Combination of Processes

No objectives at Level B.

Fractions

After completing this study guide, you will be able to:
1. divide objects and sets in half.
2. divide objects and sets into thirds.
3. divide objects and sets into fourths.

Decimal Fractions

No objectives at Level B.

Measurement

After completing this study guide, you will:
  1. know that we measure some things with a one-foot ruler. You should know that a one-foot ruler measures twelve inches and that a yardstick measures three feet. You should learn some words used to compare objects. You should also learn to identify one dozen and one-half dozen objects.

Money

After completing this study guide, you will be able to:
1. recognize the value of the penny, nickel, and dime.
2. match coins with numerical value and understand the uses of the word "cent".
3. recognize the quarter. You should also be able to understand the value of pennies, nickels, dimes, and quarters and be able to use the ¢ sign.

Time

After completing this study guide, you will be able to:
1. know the position of the 12 numerals on a clockface. You should know that the larger hand of the clock points to 12 at the hour and the shorter hand shows the hour.
2. know that at the half hour the larger hand of the clock points to 6 and the shorter hand shows the half hour. You should also know what is meant by the terms "after" and "before" the hour.

Geometry

After completing this study guide, you will be able to:
1. choose a circle, square, rectangle, or triangle from a group of shapes.

2. draw line segments by connecting points, complete patterns.
3. tell whether curves are closed or not closed, and should also be able to match names and forms of cubes, cones, spheres, and cylinders.

Special Topics

No objectives at Level B.

LEVEL C

Numeration

After completing this study guide, you will be able to:
1. read and write numerals 1-200. You should be able to fill in a sequence of numbers from any starting point.
2. supply a number one more, less, or between 1-200.
3. complete exercises for skip-counting by 2's, 5's, and 10's to 200.

Place Value

After completing this study guide, you will be able to:
1. identify place value of the units and tens up to 100. You should also be able to use the smaller-than and larger-than signs. ($<$, $>$).
2. identify and write in column units, tens, and hundreds. You should be able to use expanded notation in writing the place value of numbers.
3. use expanded notation in identifying place value meaning of numerals. You should also be able to write a numeral for problems using expanded notation.

Addition

After completing this study guide, you will be able to:
1. correctly add 50 addition facts in five minutes.
2. add two numbers with sums to 20.
3. add two addends which do not require carrying and check an addition problem by adding in reverse direction.
4. use the signs $<$, $=$, or $>$ in two-step equations combining addition and subtraction facts.
5. work column addition using two or more addends without carrying.

Subtraction

After completing this study guide, you will be able to:
1. pass a timed test on 50 of the subtraction facts in five minutes.
2. find the differences for subtraction fact statements. You should be able to work problems written in both horizontal and vertical form working with minuends to 18.
3. subtract two digits from two digits with no regrouping.

Multiplication

After completing this study guide, you will be able to:
1. multiply using sets through the 5's. You should be able to pass a timed test on the multiplication tables 1's through 5's.

Division

After completing this study guide, you will be able to:
1. work simple division problems using sets. You will also be able to pass a 5 minute timed test on the division facts through the 5's.

Combination of Processes

After completing this study guide, you will be able to:
1. add or subtract as indicated by the + or − sign.
2. find the sums and differences for problems.
3. solve one-step problems involving adding and subtracting values in money, time, and measurement.
4. use greater-than (>), less-than (<), equal (=), and unequal (≠) symbols to show relationship between a combination of numbers, addition and subtraction expressions.

Fractions

After completing this study guide, you will be able to:
1. divide objects into halves (1/2), thirds (1/3), and fourths (1/4).
2. divide a set of objects into halves, thirds, fourths, and label them as 1/2, 1/3, 1/4 of the whole set.
3. recognize, identify, and write different names for the fractions 1/2, 1/3, and 1/4.

Decimal Fractions

No objectives at Level C.

Measurement

After completing this study guide, you will be able to:
1. use an inch ruler for measuring to the nearest inch.
2. use the foot ruler and yardstick for: converting inches to feet, feet to inches, and feet to yards; recognizing the smallest and greatest length when given two lengths and for measuring inches, feet, and yards.

Money

After completing this study guide, you will be able to:
1. know the value of a nickel, a penny, and a dime. You should also be able to use a penny, nickel, and dime in counting money.
2. know the value of pennies, nickels, and dimes. You should be able to make purchases using dimes and counting by tens. You should learn and know the value of a quarter and use it in counting money.
3. understand the value of pennies, nickels, dimes, quarters, half dollars. You should be able to relate each coin mentioned above with its value.
4. solve money sentences without the use of illustrations, add and subtract money problems using the cents sign and the dollar mark.

Time

After completing this study guide, you will be able to:
1. write time for the time given on clock faces using the vertical dots (9:15), and tell time to within five (5) minutes.
2. write time shown by clocks, draw hands on clocks to show time using the minute hand and the hour hand, tell the hour, the half-hour, and the quarter-hour.
3. tell Noon, A.M., and P.M. and be able to tell the differences between A.M. and P.M.
4. know the days of the week, how many days are in a week, month, and year; know the months of the year and how many months are in a year; know the four parts, or seasons, of the year.

5. work with a calendar using the days of a week and the months of a year.

Geometry

After completing this study guide, you will be able to:
1. recognize and name sphere, cube, cone, cylinder, and rectangular prism.

Special Topics

After completing this study guide, you will be able to:
1. write Roman Numerals to 30 and convert Arabic Numerals to Roman Numerals up to 30.

LEVEL D

Numeration

After completing this study guide, you will be able to:
1. read and write numerals to 1,000 starting from any point.
2. skip count by 3's, 4's, 5's, 10's, 100's, and 1,000's (or any other number) beginning from any point.

Place Value

After completing this study guide, you will be able to:
1. identify the place value of units, tens, hundreds, and thousands, digits in numbers to 1,000 by writing the place value in words or numbers when given the digit, and by giving the digit when the place value is specified.
2. place < or > between two numbers to 1,000.
3. write numerals in expanded notation up to 1,000; regroup and rename numerals to 1,000.

Addition

After completing this study guide, you will be able to:
1. complete a 5-minute timed test on the 100 addition facts with 100% accuracy and identify all vocabulary words given as a review.
2. do column addition with two addends and three or more digit numbers which do not require carrying; check addition problems by adding in reverse direction.

3. find a missing addend within a column of numbers when the sum is given; identify the vocabulary words given.
4. identify and give examples of the terms named in this study guide. They are all related to addition.
5. add, carrying to tens place with two or more addends and sums up to 200.
6. add, carrying from tens to hundreds using three-digit numerals and two or more addends.
7. carry tens and hundreds, using three-digit numerals with or without regrouping using two or more addends.
8. find sums in column addition using two or more addends of one or more digits carrying when necessary.

Subtraction

After completing this study guide, you will be able to:
1. complete 100 subtraction facts to 20 in less than ten minutes.
2. subtract using two or more digits with no borrowing.
3. subtract using borrowing (regrouping) from the tens place in problems with two digits.
4. subtract using borrowing from tens and hundreds places in problems with three digits.
5. borrow from the tens and hundreds places in numbers with three digits.

Multiplication

After completing this study guide, you will be able to:
1. use repeated addition to solve multiplication problems.
2. explain the concept of multiplication by joining equivalent groups or sets without using repeated addition.
3. recognize the special property of 0 (zero) and 1 (one) as factors in multiplication.
4. pass a five-minute test covering 50 of the multiplication facts from 0's through 9's.
5. fill in the frame or blank with a missing factor.
6. use the multiplication terms given in the vocabulary study.

Division

After completing this study guide, you will be able to:
1. divide a set into subsets.

2. multiply facts to solve division problems, showing that division is an inverse operation of multiplication.
3. identify and use the terms: product, factor, quotient, divisor, dividend, and division.
4. complete division facts through $81 \div 9$.

Combination of Processes

After completing this study guide, you will be able to:
1. find sums and differences of numbers to 500 without regrouping (money, time, and measurement units).
2. find sums and differences of numbers to 500, regrouping to the hundreds place (money, time, and measurement units).
3. recognize the multiplication sign ($\times$) and the division sign ($\div$) and solve problems using these signs.
4. solve one-or two-step word problems in subtraction and addition.
5. use the following operational signs in problems: $<$, $>$, $=$, and $\neq$.

Fractions

After completing this study guide, you will be able to:
1. identify and write different names for the same simple fraction. Ex: $1/5 = 2/10$; $1/6 = 2/12$; $1/8 = 2/16$; $2/3 = 4/6$; $3/4 = 9/12$.
2. divide sets of objects into fractional parts.
3. add any two fractions with the same denominator.
4. subtract like fractions.

Decimal Fractions

No objectives at Level D.

Measurement

After completing this study guide, you will be able to:
1. convert inches to feet and yards; feet to yards and inches; and yards to feet and inches; and to solve word problems relating to inches, feet, and yards.
2. recognize and use liquid measure: cups, pints, quarts, half-gallons, and gallons.
3. solve word problems dealing with liquid measurement.

4. measure to the nearest inch, 1/2-inch, and 1/4-inch with your ruler and yardstick.

Money

After completing this study guide, you will be able to:
1. identify the half-dollar and dollar, find value, and use dollar sign and cent mark.
2. give the total value of coins and bills.
3. write money value using cent mark and dollar sign.
4. identify change in coins.
5. solve one-step word problems involving money.

Time

After completing this study guide, you will be able to:
1. give hours earlier and hours later from any hour given on a clock; tell number of hours between two given hours.
2. add and subtract minutes on the clock.
3. add and subtract minutes and hours; give earlier and later time when given specific time.
4. read and solve problems which deal with time.
5. know about hours, minutes, and seconds. The second hand will be presented in this study guide. There is also included the story of time and a time game.

Geometry

After completing this study guide, you will be able to:
1. recognize and identify open curves, closed curves, square corners, points on a line, and line segments.

Special Topics

After completing this study guide, you will be able to:
1. write the Roman Numerals 1 to 100.
2. read thermometers and record temperature using the degree symbol.
3. read, draw, and solve problems relating to bar graphs, line graphs, and picture graphs.

LEVEL E

Numeration

After completing this study guide, you will be able to:
1. count, read, and write numerals to 1,000,000 from any starting point
2. identify odd and even numbers; state and use the rule concerning odd and even numbers for addition, subtraction, and multiplication of two numbers.
3. round numbers to tens, hundreds, and thousands for comparing and estimating answers.
4. write two, three, four, or more digits in words.

Place Value

After completing this study guide, you will be able to:
1. identify place value digits to 1,000,000 and write numerals in expanded notation and in place value columns; and to identify numerals from expanded notation and place value columns.
2. use the signs to show relationship between two numbers to 1,000,000.
3. use multiples of ten to generalize known multiplication facts.

Addition

After completing this study guide, you will be able to:
1. do column addition with and without carrying using three or more digit numbers and two or more addends.
2. use the commutative principle of addition as a method of checking two or more place numbers.
3. add with carrying four or more place numbers with two addends.

Subtraction

After completing this study guide, you will be able to:
1. subtract with borrowing in four or more place numbers; and to use borrowing in problems using dollars and cents.

Multiplication

After completing this study guide, you will be able to:
1. answer the multiplication facts correctly in 5 minutes.
2. use repeated addition to solve multiplication problems for a one place number times one, two, three place numbers; and to multiply by tens, hundreds, and thousands using one or two digit factors.
3. explain and use the commutative principle for multiplication to solve problems with a one-place factor: Ex: $17 \times 9 = 9x$____.
4. perform multiplication with a one-digit factor times a two-digit factor. Ex:
$$\begin{array}{r} 28 \\ \times\ 9 \\ \hline 252 \end{array}$$
5. multiply a one-digit factor times a three- or more digit factor. Ex:
$$\begin{array}{r} 128 \\ \times\ 7 \\ \hline \end{array} \qquad \begin{array}{r} 4567 \\ \times\ 4 \\ \hline \end{array}$$
6. find the squares of the numbers 1-9 and write numbers in exponential form identifying the base and exponent.
7. multiply a two-digit number by a two-digit number. Ex:
$$\begin{array}{r} 68 \\ \times\ 43 \\ \hline \end{array}$$

Division

After completing this study guide, you will be able to:
1. complete 50 to 100 division facts using division sign ($\div$) or bridge process $5\overline{)\ 10}^{\ 2}$ within five to ten minutes.
2. do division with a one- or two-digit divisor and two- or more digit dividend, with no remainder.
3. do division with or without remainders with one- or two-digit division and two- or three-digit dividends.
4. do division with or without remainders for one- or two-digit divisors and two- or more digit dividends.
5. check division with remainders for one- or two-digit divisors and two- or more dividends.

Combination of Processes

After completing this study guide, you will be able to:
1. have a complete review of carrying in addition and borrowing in subtraction.
2. solve addition, subtraction, multiplication, and division equations using a letter as a variable (n, m, a, b, x, y, etc.).
3. supply the missing sign ($<$, $>$, $=$, $\neq$) for combinations of $+$, $-$, $\times$, or $\div$; and be able to solve problems with multi-operations.
4. find averages using addition and division.
5. solve one- or two-step word problems with addition, multiplication, subtraction, and division.

Fractions

After completing this study guide, you will be able to:
1. reduce fractions to the lowest terms.
2. find a fractional part of any whole number.
3. identify fractional parts by the proper terms. Ex: numerator, denominator.
4. add two or more fractions with like denominators, subtract like-fractions and reduce the answers to lowest terms.

Decimal Fractions

After completing this study guide, you will be able to:
1. know the definitions and uses of the following vocabulary: decimal, whole number, tenth, hundredth; and to convert fractions to decimal fractions whose denominators are tens or hundreds.
2. add two or more addends with whole numbers and decimals to the hundredths place.
3. subtract two numbers with whole numbers and decimals to the hundredths place (with borrowing).

Measurement

After completing this study guide, you will be able to:
1. solve problems requiring conversion of tons into pounds, into ounces, and know the equivalent measures of ounces to pounds and pounds to tons.

2. add, subtract, and multiply denominate numbers using regrouping in order to combine the same units of measurement.
3. use the equivalent measures—feet, rod, yard, mile—and solve problems using these conversions.

Money

After completing this study guide, you will be able to:
1. identify change in coins with purchase amounts up to $10.00.
2. total purchases with total amounts up to $20.00 and count out change starting with the total value of the purchase.
3. add and subtract money values, two or more, using cent and decimal notation with carrying and borrowing.
4. multiply and divide money values using the dollar sign and decimal point.

Time

After completing this study guide, you will be able to:
1. be familiar with time zones of the United States, increase your knowledge of the calendar, and add and subtract problems involving time.

Geometry

After completing this study guide, you will be able to:
1. name points in a line and recognize that the dot is used as a representation of a point; identify mid-point and end points of a line segment; name a line segment by its end points and a line by the two points on it.
2. identify a right angle and name angles by three points; identify and draw lines which are perpendicular.
3. recognize simple geometric figures, equilateral, right triangle, and quadrilateral.
4. identify lines which look parallel and draw parallel lines; identify intersecting lines, define the point of intersection, compare parallel and intersecting lines and explain the difference between line and line segment.
5. use a compass to draw circles and identify the following terms: radii, radius, diameter, compass, chord, circumference.

Special Topics

After completing this study guide, you will be able to:
1. write and recognize the seven (7) symbols in the Roman system of numerals: I = 1, V = 5, X = 10, L = 50, C = 100, D = 500, M = 1000.
2. read and draw bar graphs, line graphs, and pictographs.

LEVEL F

Numeration

After completing this study guide, you will be able to:
1. round numbers to the nearest thousands, ten thousands, and millions for estimating answers in problem form and word problem form.
2. write numerals for 5, 6, or more place numbers; and write the words for 5, 6, or more place numbers.

Place Value

After completing this study guide, you will be able to:
1. chart large numbers by the place value of each digit; and work with large numbers including billions and trillions.
2. write 10 as a power and identify the base and exponent or power of a term.
3. use exponents to name certain numerals and as a way to shorten a numeral.

Addition

After completing this study guide, you will be able to:
1. add, using carrying, with 3 or more place numbers and more than two addends.

Subtraction

After completing this study guide, you will be able to:
1. subtract using borrowing (regrouping) with four or more digits; using dollars and cents. This study guide also contains a review of previous levels.

Multiplication

After completing this study guide, you will be able to:
1. solve problems using the multiplication algorithm for a one-digit number times a two- or more digit number.
2. multiply a two-digit number by a two-digit number; be familiar with using the commutative principle for multiplication to solve problems, two places times two places.
3. use the associative principle to simplify multiplication of one- and two-digit numbers.
4. use the distributive principle to simplify multiplication of one- and two-digit numbers.
5. use the multiplication algorithm for a two-digit number times a two- or more digit number.
6. multiply three digits by three or more digits.

Division

After completing this study guide, you will be able to:
1. divide with a two place divisor which is a multiple of ten.

    Ex:
$$20\overline{)105}\begin{array}{r}5\ r\ 5\\\hline\end{array}$$

$$\begin{array}{r}5\ r\ 5\\20\overline{)105}\\\underline{100}\\5\end{array}$$

2. divide with two place divisors and check each problem by using multiplication.
3. work long division using three-digit divisors with three or more dividends with or without remainders.

Combination of Processes

After completing this study guide, you will be able to:
1. add, subtract in all directions using borrowing and carrying.
2. multiply and divide using numbers to 1,000,000.
3. supply the missing sign $<$, $>$, $=$, or $\neq$ in add, subtract, multiply, and divide problems with numbers to 1,000,000.
4. solve one and two step word problems including fractions and also the money, time, measurement units. Problems involve add, subtract, multiply, and divide.

Fractions

After completing this study guide, you will be able to:
1. add and subtract fractions with unlike denominators, and mixed numbers.
2. multiply fractions by fractions or whole numbers and reduce the product to lowest terms.
3. divide whole numbers or fractions with fractions and reduce the quotients to lowest terms.
4. think through and solve word problems using fractions.

Decimal Fractions

After completing this study guide, you will be able to:
1. identify place value of decimals to the thousandths place; convert fractions to decimals (tenths, hundredths, thousandths); add and subtract decimal numbers with whole numbers and decimals to the thousandths place.
2. multiply a decimal number times a whole number and a one or two place decimal number times a one or more place decimal number.
3. divide a decimal by a whole number and decimals by decimals to the thousandths place.
4. convert fractions to decimals which are *not* tenths, hundredths, or thousandths.
5. convert fractions and decimals to percent and percent to fractions and decimals; and find percents of numbers.

Measurement

After completing this study guide, you will be able to:
1. work problems converting measures by adding, subtracting, and multiplying with the common measures (length, weight, liquid, and dry).
2. have a workable knowledge of measuring time, distance, and speed.

Money

No objectives at Level F.

Time

After completing this study guide, you will be able to:
1. add and subtract measurements of time with regrouping; become familiar with the term "clock arithmetic".

Geometry

After completing this study guide, you will be able to:
1. find perimeters of squares, triangles, quadrilaterals, and polygons by measuring.
2. use square inch model to find areas of simple plane figures and solve simple area problems and make conversions among square units.
3. use a one-cubic inch square as a model to find volumes of simple solids; solve simple volume problems.
4. identify the following: trapezoid, pentagon, hexagon, and other polygons.
5. identify and locate the following parts of a circle: center, radius, diameter, chord, arc, and semicircle.
6. have a workable knowledge of the following: identifying a "ray" as a line segment with one endpoint and extending indefinitely in the other direction; measuring a line segment to the nearest 1/8 and 1/16 of an inch; using a compass to bisect a line segment and identifying the vertex of a triangle or angle.

Special Topics

After completing this study guide, you will be able to:
1. identify "ratio" and work simple problems.
2. use your knowledge of ratio to recognize and identify a ratio proportion equation.
3. read, draw, and use various types of graphs and charts: bar graphs, pictographs, line graphs, circle graphs.
4. use the bar scale to calculate the distance between points on a map; use multiplication and addition to determine distances.

Appendix B

GRAMMAR SKILLS CONTINUUM

LEVEL A

Punctuation

After completing this study guide, you should be able to:
1. find the period at the end of a sentence.
2. write a period at the end of a sentence.
3. find the question mark at the end of a sentence.
4. write the question mark at the end of a sentence.
5. find the exclamation point at the end of a sentence.
6. write the exclamation point at the end of a sentence.
7. find quotation marks that show when someone is speaking.
8. find the commas in a sentence.

Alphabetizing

After completing this study guide, you should be able to:
1. match pictures with beginning sounds.
2. write the name of the letter for beginning sounds of pictures.

Capitalization

After completing this study guide, you should be able to:
1. capitalize the first word in a sentence.
2. capitalize the names of people.
3. capitalize the days of the week, months of the year, and the holidays.
4. capitalize the names of cities and states.
5. capitalize the greeting and closing in a letter.

Abbreviations

No skills identified yet.

Organizing Skills

After completing this study guide, you should be able to:
1. complete a simple list.
2. tell things that happened in order.
3. put pictures in order.
4. tell a story in order.
5. write a story in order.

Dictionary Skills

No skills identified yet.

LEVEL B

Punctuation

After completing this study guide, you should be able to:
1. find and use a period at the end of a sentence.
2. find and write a question mark at the end of an asking sentence.
3. find and use a comma between the city and the state.
4. find and use an exclamation point.
5. find and use an apostrophe in a contraction.

Alphabetizing

After completing this study guide, you should be able to:
1. place words in alphabetical order by the first letter of the word.
2. find words in a beginning dictionary.
3. locate names and numbers in a telephone directory.

Capitalization

After completing this study guide, you should be able to:
1. use capital letters to begin the names of streets, cities, towns, and states.
2. use capital letters at the beginning of a sentence.
3. use a capital letter to name people.
4. use a capital letter for the days of the week, months of the year, and holidays.

5. use a capital letter for the pronoun "I".
6. use capital letters in titles of books and stories.
7. use capital letters in titles (Mr., Mrs., Miss, Dr., etc.)

Abbreviations

After completing this study guide, you should be able to:
1. abbreviate the days of the week.
2. abbreviate the months of the year.
3. abbreviate streets, roads, avenues, and routes.

Organizing Skills

After completing this study guide, you should be able to:
1. make a list of ideas and things.
2. use your name and the date correctly at the top of your paper.

Dictionary Skills

No skills identified yet.

LEVEL C

Punctuation

After completing this study guide, you should be able to:
1. use a period after abbreviations and after initials.
2. write sentences using a question mark correctly.
3. use correct punctuation in writing a date.
4. use a comma to separate city and state.
5. identify errors in punctuation in a given letter or story.
6. punctuate a sentence with quotation marks for conversation and dialogues.
7. use a hyphen to show a word break at the end of a line.
8. use a colon correctly after the greeting in a business letter.

Alphabetizing

After completing this study guide, you should be able to:
1. put words into alphabetical order according to the first letter of the word.
2. locate names and numbers in a telephone directory.

Capitalization

After completing this study guide, you should be able to:
1. write sentences beginning each with a capital letter.
2. capitalize initials and titles (including Mr., Mrs., Miss).
3. capitalize the names of streets, cities, and states.
4. capitalize names of persons, holidays, days of the week and months, the first word and important words in the title of a story, poem, song, or book.

Abbreviations

After completing this study guide, you should be able to:
1. write the abbreviations for the days of the week and the months of the year.
2. write the abbreviations for streets, roads, avenues, and states.

Organizing Skills

After completing this study guide, you should be able to:
1. use the correct heading on your daily work.
2. use the correct form in writing a letter.
3. list in a given order.
4. arrange questions into appropriate categories.
5. arrange questions or subtitles under main ideas.
6. outline two or three main headings.

Dictionary Skills

No skills identified yet.

LEVEL D

Punctuation

After completing this study guide, you should be able to:
1. use the hyphen to show a break at the end of a sentence.
2. use a colon after the greeting in a business letter.
3. use quotation marks to enclose dialogue in conversation.
4. apply an exclamation point in sentences when appropriate.
5. use the period after abbreviations and initials.

6. use the question mark after an interrogative sentence.
7. use the comma correctly in a given paragraph.

Alphabetizing

After completing this study guide, you should be able to:
1. alphabetize by the second and third letters.
2. locate words in the index and glossary.

Capitalization

After completing this study guide, you should be able to:
1. use the rules of capitalization in correcting a paragraph or story.
2. use capitalization in writing proper nouns (persons, days, holidays, titles, streets, states, etc.).
3. use capitalization correctly in outlining.
4. capitalize the first word of a quotation.
5. capitalize the titles of stories, poems, songs, and books.
6. capitalize the greeting and closing in a letter.
7. capitalize the pronoun "I".

Abbreviations

After completing this study guide, you should be able to write a paragraph or story using abbreviations where needed.

Organizing Skills

After completing this study guide, you should be able to write a simple outline with two or three main headings.

Dictionary Skills

After completing this study guide, you should be able to:
1. use a standard dictionary and glossary.
2. use accent marks for correct pronunciation for given words.
3. identify and use diacritical marks as aids in pronunciation.
4. use the dictionary to correctly syllabicate given words.

LEVEL E

Punctuation

After completing this study guide, you should be able to:
1. identify and use a comma in a direct address.
2. use a comma after yes and no.
3. use quotation marks to identify titles of stories, poems, magazine articles, etc.
4. use punctuation rules in direct quotations.
5. use the hyphen when needed to divide words and combine special compound words (merry-go-round).
6. identify errors in punctuation in a given paragraph or story.
7. punctuate given sentences correctly using periods, commas, question marks, and/or exclamation points.

Alphabetizing

After completing this study guide, you should be able to:
1. use the alphabet to locate words in an individual wordbook.
2. use the alphabet to locate information in a table of contents, index, glossary, dictionary or reference book.

Capitalization

After completing this study guide, you should be able to:
1. identify errors in capitalization in a given business letter.
2. capitalize proper nouns in a given story.
3. use capitalization in outlining.
4. capitalize the first word of a quotation.
5. capitalize the titles for stories, poems, songs, and books.
6. capitalize the pronoun "I".
7. capitalize the greeting and closing in a letter.
8. capitalize designated parts of the country and world.

Abbreviations

After completing this study guide, you should be able to write sentences and/or paragraphs using given abbreviations.

Organizing Skills

After completing this study guide, you should be able to:
1. outline a story using two or three main headings as well as two or three subheadings.
2. write an outline for a given selection to show main ideas and supporting details.
3. write a topic outline for two or more paragraphs.

Dictionary Skills

After completing this study guide, you should be able to:
1. use a standard dictionary or glossary.
2. use accent marks for correct pronunciation of given words.
3. use the dictionary to correctly syllabicate given words.
4. identify and use diacritical marks as an aid to pronunciation.

LEVEL F

Punctuation

After completing this study guide, you should be able to:
1. use a quotation mark to identify titles of stories, poems, magazine articles, etc.
2. use a colon to introduce a series of words or phrases.
3. separate two closely related independent clauses with a semicolon.
4. correct errors of punctuation in a given business letter.
5. punctuate quotations correctly.

Alphabetizing

After completing this study guide, you should be able to:
1. use the card catalog.
2. use simple cross-referencing to file stories, reports, projects, pictures, or letters.

Capitalization

After completing this study guide, you should be able to:
1. identify errors in capitalization in a given story or letter.
2. use capitalization rules in direct quotations in written conversations.

3. use capitalization rules in sentences containing quotations.
4. use capitalization rules to write titles of books, poems, songs and stories.
5. apply the rules of capitalization to a given list of regions of the country, trade names, and names of documents.

Abbreviations

After completing this study guide, you should be able to write letters, paragraphs, and stories using abbreviations correctly.

Organizing Skills

After completing this study guide, you should be able to:
1. write an outline with two or three main headings and two or three subheadings.
2. write a topic outline for two or more paragraphs.

INDEX